Poems From My Heart

Poems From My Heart

by
PHYLLIS C. MICHAEL

ZONDERVAN PUBLISHING HOUSE
GRAND RAPIDS, MICHIGAN

To
my sons
ROBERT *and* KEITH
who have been the inspiration
for many of these lines

Acknowledgments

Special acknowledgment is made to the following:

The Rodeheaver Hall-Mack Company for permission to reprint the poem, "Today Is the Day," copyright 1962.

The Lillenas Publishing Company for permission to use "Close to Mom," also the poems "Golden Years," "Through the Years," and "Sharing the Years" which are copyright 1962 in *Special Events*.

Singspiration, Inc., for permission to use the poems "Others," "This I Ask," "I Do Not Fear Tomorrow," and "God's Gardener." © 1964 by Singspiration, Inc. All rights reserved.

Ideals Publishing Company for making available "The Huskin' Bee," copyright 1961; "Log Cabin Style," copyright 1963; "At Apple Parin' Time," copyright 1964; also the many other poems contained in this volume which are scheduled to appear in future issues of *Ideals* Magazine.

CONTENTS

ALPHABETICAL INDEX

INSPIRATIONAL

I Do Not Fear Tomorrow

I do not fear tomorrow
   For I have lived today
And though my course was stormy,
   My Pilot knew the way.

I do not fear tomorrow —
   I shall not sail alone.
The same true Pilot shall be with me
   For He never forsakes His own.

I do not fear tomorrow!
   If the sails set east or west,
On sea or safe in harbor,
   In Him, secure, I rest.

Dollars and Sense

Just what can money buy? A store
Of food and clothes and land — what more?

What then can I use to buy good health?
I can't buy that with all the world's wealth.
Can money buy just one true friend?
The kind on whom I can always depend?
With what can I buy true love and laughter,
True happiness here and in the Hereafter?

Can I buy your smile, the touch of your hand?
It's worth more than all the gold in this land!
Can I buy the sweet peace that I always feel
When I kiss Baby Ann good night and then kneel
To ask God to guard and to guide us all?
Don't I know that somehow He'll answer my call?

Money can't buy such things, Lord, please
Teach me how to be truly worthy of these.

All Together

How grand when the whole fam'ly
  Sits down at the table
And eats fresh roast turkey
  As much as they're able!
There's 'taters an' 'maters
  An' gravy an' fillin' —
Oh, let me tell you
  It surely is thrillin'!
There's cranberry sauce
  An' pie, mince an' cherry
But best of all
  Those voices, how merry!

How grand when the whole fam'ly
  Sits down at the table
An' eats ev'ry crumb
  As much as they're able;
How grand to be the mother
  Of such a fine brood!
How grand that God gave us
  Each other and food!

Lord, Make Me Worthy

If I can live and laugh and love
In such a way each day
That those who then belong to me
(Though I am old and gray)
Can step up proudly anywhere
(And though I never coax)
Say fittingly to those we meet,
"*This* is my mother, folks,"
Then this is all I ask —
Lord, *this* is all I ask.

It's Easy to Understand

It's easy for me to understand
Why God loves each of us so much
Regardless of what we do or say
Regardless of race or creed and such.

It's easy for me to understand
For I have wonderful children, too;
And while my love must be far less
For them, there's nothing I wouldn't do.

It's easy for me to understand
When one of us has lost his way
How the tender Shepherd cannot rest
Till we're back in the fold e'er close of day.

It's easy for me to understand
Why a Heavenly Father can forgive,
For I, in my poor human style,
Love each and shall as long as I live.

It's easy for me to understand
How pained God is when we do wrong
For oh, how often I have wept
For mine and oh, some nights how long!

Yes, it's easy for me to understand
Why God loves each little child, indeed,
I know how precious is each little sheep
For I have lambs of my own to feed.

You Two As One

May He who marks the sparrow's fall
And watches surely over all
Keep you within His tender care
And bless each moment that you share.

Since She Is There

She was always lending a hand,
Always willing to understand,
Always noble, kind-hearted and true;
She was always smiling, too,
That cheerful cozy smile;
Always going the second mile
To bear much more than her share
Of another's burden of care.

A staunch and loyal friend,
She had courage and faith to the end;
She toiled not to get, but to give,
And that's the way she will live
Within our hearts forever.
For a little while we must sever
Our precious earthly bond,
But she is just beyond.

It's just one breath away
From here to There, so let's say,
"Though we shall miss her face,
For no one can take her place,
Very soon we shall meet again
In the land where there is no pain,
For heaven is so much nearer,
Yes, heaven is so much dearer,
Since she is there."

My Life Is a Book

My life is a book, a wonderful book
    Whose pages are etched in pure gold,
All done by a hand, a dear, tiny hand
    Which God gave me one day — to hold.

My life tells the tale of a fond mother's hopes,
    Of faith and of love without measure;
Each page now reveals some dream we once shared,
    Just me and my one perfect treasure.

My life is a book, a wonderful book,
    Made precious down through the years;
Each chapter's engraved on this old heart of mine
    And each day some new joy appears.

Others

Lord, give me an understanding heart —
A broader point of view;
Show me the way to be thoughtful and kind
In all I say and do.

Lord, give me an understanding heart —
Let me feel my brother's need;
Send words, as manna, down from above
That I his soul may feed.

Lord, give me an understanding heart —
Wake me to another's pain;
Let me walk in the garden awhile hand in hand
With him, this day, in the rain.

Lord, give me an understanding heart —
This the one treasure I ask;
Let me do what I can for my neighbor today
Without thinking it too great a task.

Tiny Little Feet

Eager,
Tiny little feet!
Restless and happy
To be on the go!
Does a hard, dusty road
Lie ahead for you?
How merciful
You should not know!

Eager,
Tiny little feet!
God keep them always
Through each day
Eager to do
Thy precious will —
Happy,
Each step of the way.

A Table Blessing

May all who sit at this table
Feel the warmth and the glow
Of a truly happy household —
One it's a joy to know.

May all who sit at this table
Share and be content;
May they see a true reflection
Of other days well spent.

May all who sit at this table
Find friendliness and cheer
And a special kind of blessing
Because God, too, dwells here.

If You Believe

The thorns we see just up ahead
God knows will be a rose instead;

He sees our needs from up above
And we can safely trust His love!

What seems just now a cross to bear
May be, in truth, a crown to wear;

So walk by faith and not by sight,
Trust God to lead through day or night,

His perfect peace you shall receive
If you believe — if you believe.

With God's Help

How many cut fingers and bruised knees, I wonder
    Have I painted or bandaged or kissed?
I know if I counted each one of them over,
    I'd have a fairly long list.

Dear Lord, since the children are taller and stronger
    And hearts bruise more quickly than knees
Without interfering or seeming unkind,
    Some day may I learn to mend these?

Without a Smile

This world would be a desert drear
    Without the wonderful smile
Of a wee tiny lass or a wee tiny lad
    In their own inimitable style.

This world would be a prison wall,
    The darkest shade of night
Without the smile of a little child,
    God's own pure shining light.

Home Blessing

God bless this home
   That's all I ask
And help me count it
   A worthy task
To fix and bake
   And wash each dish
And listen to
   Each childish wish
This morning.

God bless this home
   Oh, may I say
When evening shadows
   Come my way,
"My fam'ly's fine
   Lord, thanks to You,
For giving me
   These tasks to do,
This morning."

How Can I Fear Tomorrow?

I've had a rich life in so many ways,
   A home and a fam'ly inside it to love,
Friends, spring and summer, to blame or to praise
   And abundant faith in the good Lord above.

Oh, yes, I've had pain — I've suffered some, too!
   Fate has brought me many a care;
But I've weighed them in the balance and found it true
   God was always right there.

The good far outweighed the heartaches — the bad,
   And Time has veiled each tear.
As I face each tomorrow, there's *so* much I've had,
   How *can* I ever fear?

God Bless Your Home

God bless your home and dwell within,
　　Within each room you share;
Oh, may you feel His guiding hand,
　　His presence always there.

God bless your home with love and peace
　　His peace above all things;
God grant you faith and courage, too,
　　To share what each day brings.

God bless your home with happiness
　　The true, the noble kind;
God keep you safe within His care
　　Your ties the kind that bind.

Let Me Have Faith
(A Mother's Meditation)

When the sky is blue, an April blue, dear Lord,
Let me have faith;
When all the world seems tuned in sweet accord,
Let me have faith —
Faith like the robin in the midst of his northbound flight,
Faith that the spring must come as day follows night,
Faith that I, too, even I, am precious in Your sight,
Let me have faith.

When the sky is gray, a November gray, then, too,
Let me have faith;
When the pulse of the earth beats slower as it's bound to do,
Let me have faith —
Faith like an oak though its branches be ever so bare,
Faith that's aware some days must be less fair,
Faith that's secure, Lord, in Your all-sufficient care,
Let me have faith —
Let me have faith.

And All the Time

Many are the moments I've wasted
  In idle, bitter tears;
Many are the doubts I've sheltered
  These many selfish years;
Many are the bridges I've pictured
  Hopelessly, needlessly so
For God was watching from His window —
  And to think I didn't know.

God Is

No matter how far mortal man may probe
  Beyond our present sphere
Where life or space or stars exist
  This one great fact is clear —
    God is!

No matter what kind of new fangled things
  Man finds or learns to use
With one accord we must agree
  Within this awesome news —
    God is!

Whatever powers man may set free
  Or learn the secret of,
There is no greater power beneath
  Or anywhere above —
    God is!

Just how He moves, discerns, creates
  Is not within man's range;
But this we know without His hand
  There is no life, no change —
    God is!

Blessing

God dwell with you, within your home
  Within your hearts and minds,
And help you share each little hope,
  Each joy the other finds.

God dwell with you and bless each day
  As it unfolds for you;
May each bring nothing else but love
  And joy your whole life through.

Thy Will, Not Mine

A million times I must have prayed,
  "Dear Lord, Thy will be done";
And yet my heart is not at peace
  When storm clouds hide the sun.

Oh, could it be that what I meant
  Was *my* will, never Thine?
Dear Lord, forbid, for human eyes
  Can't see like those divine.

Cleanse Thou my heart from ev'ry doubt
  Dear Lord, *Thy* will be done!
Ah yes, ah yes! *Thy* will, not mine
  Though storm clouds hide the sun!

Somewhere behind those clouds of gray
  The sun is shining still;
Lord, give me faith, true faith to pray
  And grace to trust *Thy* will.

Lord, Bless Us

Lord of each earth, each sky, each home,
How great Thy majesty, Thy power;
Throughout all time, throughout all space
Dwell with us, here, each hour.

Lord, dwell within our home, our hearts;
Grant us true peace of mind.
Oh, make and keep us one in Thee,
Let us be the thoughtful kind.

Walk daily with each one of us
That we may feel Thee near;
Oh, keep us ever in Thy care —
These folks we hold so dear.

If I Had Wings

Oh, to have wings and fly away,
Away, away, away,
Far from each care, each heartache, each woe,
Away this very day.

But somehow in God's perfect plan
I have but hands and feet;
And so I know He must have meant
That I should calmly meet
Each jagged stone that lines my path,
Each wall that hides my view,
For it may be some little rose
Grows near my footsteps, too.
Some blossoms white may grace the wall
Where honeysuckle clings
And I should miss their sweet perfume
If I — if I had wings.

All That Matters

Twelve little dresses hang on the line;
  And shirts? I've not counted them all.
It seems that the washing never is done —
  It's like trying to move a stone wall.

But yet, when I tuck them in bed at night,
  After their evening prayers,
My Betty Jane and Danny Boy,
  I'm sure there's nothing compares
With the pride and the joy in my mother heart.
  I smile as I turn out the light;
What matter if the wash is piled sky high?
  The world *and* the wash are alright.

For Things As They Are

Just outside my windowsill
  A violet hung its head in the rain;
But then, as soon as the shower was done,
  It righted itself again.
It looked up to God and said, "Thank You, Lord,
  For sending me what is best.
The sun and the rain to make me grow
  Strong to withstand ev'ry test."

I, too, just now, would say, "Dear Lord,
  I thank You for the rain,
I thank You for sending me joy today
  And I thank You for yesterday's pain.
For to walk awhile with grief and despair
  Makes joy the sweeter by far;
It teaches me, oh it teaches me well,
  To be thankful for things as they are."

Help Wanted
(From a Diary)

The modern house is a work of art,
Ev'ry step saving gadget is there;
But give me an old fashioned, cozy house —
One with a rocking chair;
One where others have learned to pray,
One where a fond mem'ry hides
In ev'ry nook and corner about;
One where love abides;
One that contains not only the dreams
Of days that are yet to be
But also the joys of days that are passed
As a trustworthy pattern for me.
For where another has made it a home
With ties that bless and bind,
There in that house I, too, shall feel
I can knit the very same kind.

Oh, give me a house that's had ups and downs
Even as I will now;
It will help me to know that in that house
Someone found the answer somehow.
Give me the "lived in" sort of house —
It can never be lonely inside
For it's filled with faith and hope and love
And I'm such a *brand new* bride!

Forward

I cannot turn backward, I must go on
    Although the path be steep;
Oh, would that I could undo certain things,
    But yesterday's key God keeps!

I cannot turn backward — what's done is done,
    But somehow there's faith in my heart
For this morning God gave me a brand new day
    And said, "Well now, let's start."

As a Little Child

I slowly opened my weary eyes
To a morning cold and gray;
I wondered then, "Oh, what's the use
Of anything this day?"

And then I heard a little child —
His voice was filled with glee.
What can it be? What can it be
That he alone can see?

Ah, yes, he wasn't looking at
The rain a pouring down,
He wasn't drawing up his face
In a grim, unyielding frown.

He was busy building towns with blocks
And happy all the while;
No lack of faith, no little rain,
Could dampen his sweet smile.

Oh, why can't I accept the rain,
The gray days, just as he,
And question not God's perfect plan —
The things I know must be.

At the Church

I'm proud of my fam'ly, its captain, its crew;
I'm proud of each member, each good thing they do.
But never, no never do I feel quite as proud
As when we're a part of that wonderful crowd
At the church.

We sit there together right up near the front;
None of us is missing, there's no need to hunt.
There's Martha and Billy and Betty and Jill,
There's Charlie and Kathy and Nancy and Phil,
Then, of course, there's the Captain clear up at the end
And me holding Jamie just half round the bend.
I'm proud of my fam'ly, there's no greater joy
Than sharing God's blessings, each girl and each boy —
At the church.

Happiness Street

If you would live on Happiness Street
Don't judge your friends at all
Unless you judge them fair and square
And not make their good seem small.

If you would live on Happiness Street
Look for the best in each
Look for the kindness, the sweetness, the faith,
The rosy side of the peach.

If you would live on Happiness Street,
You can't be grumpy or cross,
So count each moment you spend finding fault
As vain and hopelessly lost.

Think kind thoughts, do only kind deeds
And don't be looking for a cheat;
You'll see in others just what you think —
Live on Happiness Street.

Just a Bit o' Lovin'

Just a bit o' lovin'
As you go along;
Just a bit o' changin'
Sorrow into song;
Just a bit o' helpin'
Where life's gone all wrong,
That's the kind o' livin'
Makes a man feel strong!

Just a bit o' lovin'
Just an outstretched hand;
Just a bit o' sharin'
'Cause you understand;
Just a bit o' carin'
That's what God has planned
And whether you give it or get it,
Oh, but ain't it grand?

Two Little Words

Two little words, the hardest words
In the English language to say;

Two little words, but they can bring
Oh, such wonderful pay!

Two little words! How many times
We ought to try them out!

Two little words when we kneel to pray
Or just as we walk about,

Two little words, truly spoken
Could change the fate of man;

Two little words — "I'm sorry" —
Say them — *if you can!*

Success

Success isn't reached with one mighty stride
No matter how long, no matter how wide;
Success is found only along life's road
By those who walk toward it — yes, day after day.

Success, true success, isn't pretense or sham —
Just thinking yourself, "The One Great I Am";
Success is devotion and diligence, too —
It's doing each moment the *best* you can do.

Not Forever Lost

It was better to have known just once
   Tiny arms outstretched to me;
It was better to have held you thus
   To my breast so tenderly.
It was better to have seen you there
   Oh, so happy at your play;
It was better to have loved you, dear,
   In a mother's own true way.
It was better far than never at all
   To have known a mother's bliss;
It was better far, I'm sure
   To have felt a baby's kiss.

It was better, yes, it was better —
   I really know this now
For the mem'ries I cherish of you
   Serve to help me cope somehow
With the cares in this old world
   As I go my lonely way.
It was better, yes it was better
   To have had you for a day.

As Little Birds Fly

The hardest thing mother birds must do
    Is to watch their young fly from the nest;
It's so hard to stand by as they try their wings
    Thinking that they know what's best.

But a very wise God has planned it all
    And who are we to ask why?
We, too, must stand by and let our young grow
    Stronger each time they fly.

The vict'ries they gain, the failures they meet
    Each teach them better than we;
But, oh, it's so hard to let them go
    Knowing some hardships must be.

Faith Is the Thing

No man ever climbed to lofty heights
    By thinking he couldn't do it;
But he *has* slipped backward a step or two
    By simply saying, "I knew it."

Yes, even an ant can carry a load
    Right over the ground or through it
Though it's twice his size, if he tells himself,
    "There's really nothing to it."

Faith is the thing one needs to rise
    Above one's own imperfection —
Faith in a God whose eyes are turned
    Just now in your direction.

Faith is the thing one needs to win,
    True faith and hope — never lose them;
With your hand in the Lord's, launch out in the deep,
    God gave you your talents — use them.

An Eye for an Eye

An eye for an eye and a tooth for a tooth,
At least that's what some folks say;
But wouldn't this world be a terrible place
If ev'ryone lived that way?

Oh, happy is he who knows in his heart
How to forgive and forget,
How to do good to both friend and foe —
No happier man can be met.

On Your Graduation Day

Today as you stand on life's threshold
    And face a challenge that's new,
Look forth and choose your pathway
    With care and diligence, too.

The way you take may be stony
    Quite rugged and full of cares;
But remember there's One above you
    Who knows and each burden shares.

He will give you strength for the journey
    Patience and courage too;
Let Him be your constant companion —
    He will always see you through.

As the days go by, oh, so swiftly,
    Do the very best that you can;
God has given you many talents —
    You are part of His great plan.

In this world that lies about you
    There's a corner just for you;
So keep your goal there before you
    Press onward, brave and true.

Happiness

Happiness isn't a crystal ball
Where you gaze at the future, at all — at all;

Happiness is just accepting each day
The wonderful things that come your way;

Happiness is a house anyone can build
But it's only as big any day as its filled

With laughter and love, with faith, with thanksgiving;
It's not riches or sunshine — it's a *way* of living.

Whatever's ahead, whatever's behind,
It's there on your doorstep — it's easy to find.

Happiness isn't the moon or a bright shining star,
It's the love in your heart — just where you are.

A Friend Is a Friend

A friend is a friend who's a friend when you need him,
A friend when all others pass you by;
A friend is a friend, if, in spite of your failures,
He's a friend till the day you die.

A friend is a friend if he's patient and thoughtful,
If he shows that he cares in some way;
A friend is a friend when he bids you good morning
Tomorrow the same as today.

I Watched a Miracle

I watched the dawn come shining through
This morning on my knees;
I saw the darkness change to light
As quickly as you please;
I saw the miracle of God
Before my very eyes;
How great God is, how good God is!
How wondrous and how wise!

I saw the twilight come again,
The sun sink out of sight;
And o'er the waiting earth came peace,
'Twas wrapped in softest night.
I know the sun will shine again
Tomorrow when I wake;
I watched a miracle tonight
That only God can make.

It Only Takes a Minute

It only takes a minute
To say a word of cheer;
It only takes a minute
To dry a falling tear;
It only takes a minute
To lend a helping hand;
It only takes a minute
To try to understand;
It only takes a minute
To make and keep a friend;
It only takes a minute
Some broken heart to mend;
It only takes a minute
To brighten someone's day.
Then use this very minute
Before it slips away.

HOMES

Lord, Bless Our Home

Lord, bless these sacred vows we take —
  Oh, keep us ever true;
Help us to look to Thee as one
  In all we say and do.

Lord, bless the bread we eat each day,
  Make this the bread of life;
Keep us forever in Thy care,
  Keep us from sin and strife.

Lord, bless our home with ties that bind
  Through joy or yet through woe;
Dwell Thou within our hearts, we pray,
  As moments come and go.

Lord, bless our home with perfect love,
  Bless Thou each thought and deed;
Fill both our hearts with Thy own grace.
  Unite us in our need.

Lord, bless our home, be ever near
  To guide us day by day;
Until we see Thee face to face,
  Oh, keep us in Thy way.

This Home of Ours

This home of ours — our very first home —
Might look to you quite small,
The things inside not nearly as grand
As yours at all, at all.
But this home of ours — our very first home —
Is grand enough for me.
How perfect it seems for just us two
And someday, perhaps ——— three.

Our Home

May our home be a haven
Of peace
And contentment
Knowing laughter
And love
Without strife;
May our home be a harbor
Where we find
New courage
To sail
The sea
Of life.

Home

Home! I'm as tired as I can be —
But there's Old Rover to welcome me.
"I'm glad you came," he seems to say,
"I missed you all this livelong day."
At the door stands Sue and my little son —
"Hello, sweetheart, I'm glad you're home!"
Those little arms outstretched say, "Take —
I've waited so long for you to make
A trotting horse from your big strong knee."
Oh, what a wonderful sight to see!

The smell of biscuits fills the air
And steak as I like it, medium rare;
Close by the fire is my old arm chair,
My slippers and paper, too, wait there.
Home! at last my cares are o'er!
Home! at last all is well once more!
Home! where all is ever so nice —
Ah sure and it's a bit o' God's paradise!

Be It Ever So Humble

Be it ever so humble, be it ever so grand —
Home is the best place on sea or on land.

You may sail to the south or yet to the north
Whichever way you choose, just you go forth.

Stay there and play there or work if you will,
Look all around you, live gayly, but still,

When comes the evening, the set of the sun
And a tiny wee bit of a tear has begun,

I think you'll agree, yes, gladly, with me
There's more to this rhyme than there once seemed to be.

Be it ever so humble, be it ever so grand —
Home is the best place on sea or on land.

Seems So

It may not seem like a palace to you
   This wonderful place I call home;
It's small and it's shabby to the nth degree
   But it fits me like a song fits a poem.
It has no grand entrance, no huge chandelier,
   No butler, no long winding stair;
But let me tell you when the world's got me down
   No place on this earth can compare.

It's the grandest of mansions as far as I know
   When it comes to the comfort it brings;
In fact I wouldn't want to trade it at all,
   Not even for the palace of fine kings.
It may not seem worth it to you as you look
   For it needs, well, a lot of repair;
But humble town, tumble down just as it is,
   It's *home* — it's home to me there.

Home Is Home

Home isn't exactly a thing you can buy
  Though you're ever so rich or so grand.
It may be a one room apartment upstairs,
  But it knows the touch of your hand.
It's the little toy elephant there on the sill,
  The piano, the songs that you sing,
The bouquet of zinnias you picked all yourself —
  It's the place where you feel like a king.

Home isn't the door, the ceiling, the stairs,
  Or the frame of the house at all:
It's the things all around that belong just to you
  Like Bob's picture that hangs on the wall,
The book that lies open, waiting, half read,
  The chair by the window over there,
The vase that was Grandmother Kate's long ago,
  Your collection of prized earthenware.

Home *may* be the seashore, the mountains, the farm,
  Or a path with *no* house in view;
But it's always the place where your true treasures are,
  The things that are dearest to you.
Home *could* be a palace or even a dream —
  The tablecloth gingham or lace;
But it's always the spot where your heart wants to be.
  Home — your own little place.

Your Home and My Home

Your home and my home though many miles apart,
Are one and the same thing, the cradle of the heart.

It's here we live best though in far diff'rent style;
It's here we take our troubles and change them for a smile.

Your home and my home, though here or though there,
Though castle or cottage, it's ever so fair;

And that's as it should be, to each his is best;
We're safe from life's storms in our own little nest.

Only One House Is Home

Hundreds and hundreds of interesting houses
Beckon wherever I roam;
Castles and cottages shining or shabby,
But only one house is home.

It's not what I find outside or around them,
It's not that they're big or they're small;
It's not that there's no rocking chair by the window;
It's none of these vague things at all.

It's just that the people at home are my kinfolks —
With them I don't need to pretend;
I'm just me — as I am, no better, no worse
Yet love knows no grudge, no end.

There's Mother, God bless her, and then there's our Daddy,
There's Jimmy, and Bonnie, and Sue.
Castles and cottages, shining or shabby —
Only one house will do.

It's Good to Be Home

It's good to be home! Oh, it's good to be home!
  What a wonderful, wonderful place!
I can kick off my shoes and do as I choose
  Without any thought of disgrace.

The mountains, the seashore, even cities are grand;
  What marvelous sights — to see!
But only for awhile, for by many a mile —
  Home is the best place for me.

Then Home Is Best

Home! It's beautiful in the gay dress of springtime
  With its slippers of blossoms so rare,
Its bright scarlet tulips, its pale yellow jonquils
  Blooming round our feet ev'rywhere.
The fragrance of springtime steals inside on the breezes
  That go softly floating by;
How I love it! How I cherish each fairyland moment!
  Home, and spring's cloudless sky!

Home! Summer, too, is quite welcome, I'm sure,
  With the peace of her warm lazy ways;
Underneath the branches of our big oak tree,
  That's where I spend my days.

Home! And autumn! Ah, that is still better
  With our hills and our mountains all around
Turning russet and red and some of them golden
  Ripe apples and chestnuts on the ground.

But I want to tell you, my friend, a little something,
  Yet, I think that you've already guessed;
Deep in winter, round 'bout Christmas, by your own
        cozy fireside —
  That's when home's *really* — best.

Riches or Rags

Home is not home — without a small dog
   Curled up by your favorite chair,
Just lying there hoping you'll soon walk in,
   Just waiting to welcome you there.

Home is not home without a small dog,
   No other more loyal than he;
No need to explain when things have gone wrong,
   Your heart, it's true, he can see.

Home is not home without a small dog,
   A merry little tail that wags,
A friend who adores you, just as you are,
   Riches — or rags.

To Each His Own

Home, to some, may be a window
   With violets both purple and pink;
Home, to some, may be a table
   Or a quiet nook to think;
Home, to some, may be a rocker,
   A lamp and a book to enjoy;
Home, to some may be the laughter
   Of a frolicking pint-sized boy;
Home, to some, may be the comfort
   That's found in a wee lassie's kiss;
Home, to some is a garden of roses,
   A lawn and a pathway — all this.
Ah, yes! I'll agree they're mighty important;
   But then I would choose by far
Home, to me, is the one spot on this earth
   Nearest to where *you* are.

Our House Is Not Home

Our house is not home without *you!*
What is food or laughter or books or TV?
Even friends who visit can plainly see
Our house is not home without *you.*

At Home

There's a little tyke watching eager and gay,
Nose to the window 'bout this time of the day —
At home.

There's a long winding path, roses pink and red
Climbing over a fence most as high as my head —
At home.

There's a welcome mat, too, by the door over there;
A black and white kitten curled up on the floor —
At home.

There's the smell of roast chicken and warm apple pie
And plenty of coffee if a friend should drop by —
At home.

There's Pam, in her apron What a wife! What a kiss!
What more could I ask for? I find perfect bliss —
At home.

Oh, there's pictures, there's rocking chairs, knickknacks and books,
All these and I love them though they're not much for looks —
At home.

But what I like best about the whole thing
Is the way that I feel — I'm happier than a king —
At home.

Really Home

Oh give me a home, an old fashioned home
    With geraniums in the window, three or four,
A kitchen with a clock shelf, ruffled and gay,
    And a motto hung over the door —
"God bless our home." Ah, this I insist,
    It must stay there as long as I live;
Move the organ from the parlor and the lamp from the stand
    But this one thing you must give,
An old fashioned home, the kind where love reigns,
    One where our neighbors know it;
An old fashioned home, a home where God dwells,
    One where we don't fear to show it.

Castle or Cottage

Castle or cottage, country or town,
Red brick or gray stone, white paint or brown,
Humble, unnoticed, or steeped in renown —
It's home.

It's home if you've lived there and loved it like a friend;
It's home if its mem'ries and tomorrow's dreams blend;
It's home if you're happy though you've nothing to spend —
It's home.

Castle or cottage, on hilltop or plain,
Deep in the woodland or right on North Main;
It's home if you're longing to go there again —
It's home.

It's home where the cares of the day step aside;
No need to pretend, there's nothing to hide;
It's paradise, surely, this can't be denied —
It's home.

Where I Belong

Home, to me, is my mother-in-law's place
With its chintz, its gay kitchen, its gingham, its lace,
Its old fashioned coal stove, its smell of fresh bread,
Its huge faded arm chairs, its carpet — once red.
I've lived in fine houses in many a town,
I've traveled this country both up hill and down,
But still, home, to me, is my mother-in-law's place —
I knew it the minute I saw her sweet face;
Here I've found happiness, true peace of mind,
Here love is never the make believe kind;
Here all my being seems bursting with song;
Here I feel wanted and needed — I belong.

Here to Stay

Now Sally is an alley cat
    With a patch of white on her back
That shows when she arches it a bit
    Like when Ginger steals her snack.
Oh, Ginger is a friendly dog —
    The boys brought him home one day;
He looks some like a spaniel, too,
    When he turns a certain way.

These two have shared our humble home
    For several years, I know
And home, without them, would seem quite strange,
    If one of them should go.
Ginger's learned that Sally likes the chair
    That gets the morning sun;
And Sally's learned that when Ginger barks,
    She doesn't *have to* — run.

In short, we've all got "used to" them
    And they to us, it's true;
They've pushed the portals of our hearts
    Apart and walked right through.

Just Like Mine

I want my home to be like the home
   I knew when I was small —
A home where faith was all around,
   Where love grew on each wall.
I want my child to know the peace
   I know today because
My mother took the time to pray —
   To teach me God's own laws.
I want to keep my kitchen bright,
   My table set with grace,
The kind it takes to make him feel
   He's welcome in this place.

I want to play, to take time out
   To hear each childish word;
To talk to him, to walk with him,
   Let him know he's been heard.
I want to make him feel each day
   This home is his home, too —
A place where we can share each joy,
   Each problem old or new.
I want to be there when he calls
   And yet not let him lean;
I want to watch him grow each day
   Strong, and true, and clean.

I could not ask for greater wealth
   Or greater gift to give
Than just a home like my home was
   Where this, my child, may live.

Home From College

Home from college! School is out!
And that's something you can shout about!
Mother's fixed my fav'rite pie;
Johnny says, "Oh, me! Oh, my!
Better give Sis this or that,
Never once begin a spat."
Daddy always makes a fuss,
Meets me early at the bus,
"Fran, it's good to see you, dear,
Wish that you could stay right here."

Home from college! Home at last!
All my mid-year "crams" are past;
I just want to sleep till noon,
Don't you call me — not too soon!

Home from college! Say, it's great!
But Monday I go back — I just can't wait!

We

May we be a happy family
Each moment throughout the day;
May we be a friend to each other
In ev'ry sort of way.
Though it takes a lot of planning
And a lot of praying as well,
Though it takes a lot of forgiving
And more patience than tongue can tell,
May we be a happy family
With love enough and to spare —
We and ev'ry good neighbor
Who shares our humble fare.

PARENTS

This Day

Today is the happiest day of my life —
  I saw you walk down the aisle,
Your shoulders square in your cap and gown,
  On your face the trace of a smile.

Yes, today is the happiest day of my life
  The day your daddy and I
Have looked forward to since you were just six
  How swiftly the years flew by!

I'll admit there were times, many times when the road
  Seemed long and rough up ahead;
But you buckled right in with your book and a grin —
  "I can try," was all that you said.

Now you've made it, your school days are over and done!
  Life waits at the top of the hill!
Today is the happiest day of my life;
  When I'm ninety, I'll remember it still.

What Greater Gift?

What greater gift could God give to us
Than a sweet little bundle to hold?
A tiny child of one's very own
With hair of black or of gold,
With laughing eyes which look into one's own
And a bright rosy cheek to kiss?
I thank God today for each little child,
They're one gift I wouldn't want to miss.

Prayer for Parents

Dear Heavenly Father,
Help us both to be good parents;
Let us love with a love that sees beyond
All selfish aim;
Help us learn to look to Thee each moment of our lives
For guidance
In this great task which you have given us.
Lord, may we always feel it is not only a great task
But a wonderful privilege to be
A parent.

Help us to unite our hearts and our minds
In one common goal —
The good of our family and the good we may do
For others.
In so doing, help us remember that good does not always
            consist in
Giving all and requiring nothing.
Little oaks grow strong by standing alone
Against the wind.
So, dear Lord, help us think twice before making things
Too easy
For those you have entrusted to our care.

Help us laugh the genuine laugh of
Companionship
As we work and play with our children.
Let us be a part of their lives, yet
Not such a dominant part that we hinder
Their growth.
Let us always take time to listen
To their hopes, their joys, and their troubles,
Knowing that sometimes all a child needs
Is just someone to listen
To him.

Help us not to talk
Too much
But to mean ev'ry word that we say. Let us keep
Each promise
For faith is so easily broken.

Above all, dear Father, help us keep our children
Close to You, and this
Not by our words, but by our daily living.
Keep our faith always strong
That theirs may be strong,
Also.

Give us wisdom, O Lord,
That we may teach them the joy
Of fair play
And of living both honestly and bravely
Even when the field
Is rough.
Help us teach them to love,
To be understanding, to be patient and to be
Trustworthy.
Their lives will be judged by others, but let them be
Untroubled
By what others may say. Let them know that
When evening comes
If they can kneel and truly say,
"Lord, I bring this day to You, I've done my best,"
Then this is all
Anyone
Can ask.

Now, Lord, we must go and see that the children
Are all "tucked in" and sleeping peacefully.
I don't know what else we should ask for,
But just let us do *our* best to be
The kind of parents
You
Want us to be,
Won't You, Lord?
Amen.

Parents

A parent is a thing which comes
In many varieties and colors —
Old, young, tall, short, fat, skinny,
White, black, brown, and many shades
And tones of each. They also come
In two sexes — male and female.
Some parents work in offices,
In shops, or on farms and literally thousands
Of other places. Some drive trucks and some,
Mostly in the case of the female of the species,
May be found scrubbing floors, washing windows,
Baking cakes, doing dishes, ironing clothes,
Sitting at the bedside of a sick friend,
Or traveling to any of their respective places
Of employment. Seldom, if ever, are parents found
In deep cushioned, cozy chairs,
Reading the latest lengthy novel
With a stool drawn under
Their slippered feet, for parents
Seldom find time for such —
Luxuries.

Wherever parents are found,
Somewhere in that vicinity one may also find
A child — or a dozen of them. These, too,
Come in assorted colors and sizes
And in varying degrees of dependency.
The child may be a new born infant
Who depends on his parents for all things
Except the air he breathes, or, he may have grown into
A stately professor at Yale who needs,
At the moment, very little, if any, help
Except that which is a "carry over"
From his earlier years. The latter
Cannot really be greatly discounted either
For it seems that all parents exert,
Either consciously or unconsciously,
A mighty influence on their children.

This same influence
Applied in a child's formative years
Determines, in a greater or lesser degree
What a child becomes. It seems to bear
Some direct relation to whatever his parents
Have been able to supply for him.
I do not mean materially — ah, no,
This is the least of the influences;
I do mean mentally and spiritually
For when a parent isn't working,
Or, sometimes merely *by* his working, he is shaping
The life of his child.

I have said that parents come
In many varieties, but ev'ry parent
Has one thing in common — his never dying love
For his child. This love, a parent shows
In many ways such as doing without a new refrigerator
In order that his child may have
The best clothing, schooling, equipment,
The best chance to make good in this game
Called life, and all this in the child's own
Chosen way. What's more
The peculiar part about it all
Is that parents are happiest when
They are "doing for" their children
No matter how grateful or how ungrateful;
Parents are happiest when they know
They have contributed
In the greatest possible degree
To the fullest development of
Their children. Parents want nothing,
Ask nothing but that the good Lord above
Who is the Author and Finisher of each task begun,
Give them wisdom to lead that little child
He has placed in their human hands
In paths which direct him not only
To the child's ultimate happiness
But to a station in life which is where
He may do the greatest good. In short,

Ev'ry parent wants to lead, with God's help,
His child in such a manner that this child, too,
Someday, may know the blessings of being
The kind of parent he has been —
Only better.

My Folks

Good friends are a boon
In April or June
If you wheedle them, coddle
Or coax;
But for all year round wear
There's none can compare
With those wonderful people —
My folks.

My Thanks

Dear God, I want to thank You now
    That I can proudly wear
The name of parent on my sleeve —
    No name can quite compare.
The work, the heartaches, too, are gone,
    These things when a child grows tall
Are quite forgotten through the years;
    Just love remains — that's all.

The New Look

There are many things I would do today
   But out of them all I'd like best
To stay by the side of a child at play
   And be his unseen guest.

There are many lessons not found in a book
   On faith and humility,
Lessons I could learn if I chanced to look
   Through the eyes of a child — at me.

What Is a Parent?

A parent is a thing little laddies sometimes think
   Ought not ever be around;
A necessary evil in an ever changing world
   Where such evils must abound.

A parent is a thing with a strange compelling voice
   Always saying, "Don't do that!"
Always finding useless tasks little folks must do for them
   Like a perfect autocrat!

A parent is a thing that hates a lot of noise
   And even frogs and mice;
He makes boys go to school even when they'd rather not
   And he hates to call you twice.

But a parent's sort of nice when a laddie needs a friend
   In the middle of the night
When ev'ryone's in bed and it's dark as it can be,
   Then parents are all right.

A Parent's Apology

Act I didn't go so well, did it, Son?
Somehow I missed my cue
And the lines you "ad libbed" didn't seem to fit
The situation or you.

Let's both go out and come in again —
We all have dreams in life;
The question is, then, how are they used?
As walls to build up the strife?
Or do we make of them stepping stones
Where we take each other's hand
And say, "We two can work this out
If we try to understand."

When next I hear your cue to me,
"I see it a different way,"
I won't forget my lines this time:
Proudly and firmly I'll say,
"I'll never, no never lose faith in you;
When this is over and done,
I'll be standing by as long as I live —
Call me if you need me, Son."

MOTHERS

A Mother's Prayer

May God grant you — joy,
All your life through,
Courage and strength
For each task you must do;
May God grant you — peace,
True peace and true love,
His peace and His blessing
Each day from above;
May God grant you — faith,
The kind that endures —
May His will and His way
Always be yours.

Advice From Mom
(On Her Golden Wedding Day)

If y' ain't been married fifty years
I s'pose you'll shed nigh a bucket o' tears
A learnin' you're not t' kick the traces
Each time y' run a couple o' paces;
A learnin' t' laugh, 'stead o' gettin' provoked
Cause you're only half of a team that's yoked.

But you'll learn sometime 'fore fifty years
You've got t' give an' take, my dears,
For if one tries t' pull the cart t' the right
An' 'tother pulls left with all his might,
The cart won't budge t' the east or west
Till y' both concede straight ahead is best.

Yes, you'll learn during one of those difficult years
T' head in the same direction, my dears!
Then if both o' you pull with all your might,
Your cart o' marriage will go all right;
That's why folks call it a golden weddin' —
You're hitched an' y' know which way you're headin'.

They Also Serve

They also serve who dust and sweep
And bake fresh apple pie,
Wash tiny clothes or press each dress,
Each shirt that hangs nearby.

They also serve who kiss each bruise,
Who smooth each troubled brow,
Who mend both socks and hearts with ease —
They seem to know just how.

They also serve — it's true their names
May not be seen in lights;
But oh, how much just mother means —
There are no greater heights.

Close to Mom

I'm glad that I live close to Mom
At home, yes, ev'ry day;
For I have heard there are some folks
Whose Mom lives far away.

I never could do without my Mom
And neither could Dad, I know;
Who else could find our Sunday clothes
Bake and cook or sew?

But more than that, who else would care
If I fell and hurt my knee?
Who else, when I get cold at night
Would come and cover me?

I'm glad that I live close to Mom —
I'm gladder ev'ry day;
And because she is so wonderful,
God bless her, this, I pray.

A Mother's Creed

I *believe* in little children
And in the Great Creator of this bit of art.
I *believe* in the desire of ev'ry child
To do what is basically good and right.
It is my duty as a mother to help my child
Accomplish this good by whatever means is necessary.
I *believe* in love —
I think ev'ry child, young or old, needs love.
It, therefore, becomes my privilege to give him the gift of
Love and understanding — withholding none.
I *believe* in faith — the faith of a little child
Which questions not the wisdom of the Heavenly Father;
I know I must help my child keep that faith
Throughout life's day.
I *believe* in hope — I see in my child the hope of the world.
In him and through him this great universe must become
A better place to live, perhaps, not because of any measure
Of his greatness, but because of the abundance of
His kindness and his thoughtfulness
Toward others.
I *believe* I cannot create, direct, or show by example
How life can be lived at its best
Without the help of the Father above —
His is the power, the kingdom, and the glory.
But I *believe* that because God has entrusted to my care
A little child, because He has placed this child's tiny hand
In my own, He will grant me a mother's love
Her faith, her hope, her wisdom;
And I *believe* that He will teach me how to use these virtues
If I seek each hour of the day His blessing for us both —
Mother — and child.
Amen.

To the Both of You

It's hard for a mother to share her son,
He who had been all her own;
It's hard to forfeit your claim on his love
To someone he's just lately known.
It's hard to share him when you've learned that he likes
His eggs on a piece of toast,
That he drinks his coffee hot and black,
That he wants green peas with his roast.
It's hard to share him when *you've* been the one
He brought all his troubles to,
The one who kissed away all of his tears,
The only love he knew.
It's hard to share him after all these years —
He's so much of your life a part,
It's hard when you think of the joys of the past —
It's hard when you *think* with your *heart*.

It's hard for a mother to share her son
But share him she knows she must;
And I'm glad it's you, dear, I shall share him with —
Someone I know I can trust.
I'm sure I'll learn to love you, too,
In time as he does now
Both for yourself and because you're the one
He chose from the crowd somehow.
But you, my brand new daughter-to-be,
Would you mind if just once in a while
I do things for him, bake cookies and such
In my own old fashioned style?
I promise never to steal him from you —
He's yours to keep from this day;
But just let me be to *the both of you* —
Mother in some little way.

The Greatest Gift

The world is such a wondrous place
With all its many patterned lace —
The silhouettes of stately pine
Against a sunset borderline,
The purple mountains just below,
The mirrored streams which gaily flow
Through meadowlands, the orchards, too,
Ah, yes, each thing within our view
Be it an ocean wide and deep
Or just a rose that wakes from sleep.
And I would thank the God above
For all His kindness and His love
In sending us these things so fair,
But what, I ask you, can compare
With this, the greatest gift God planned —
A mother — ah, so sweet, so grand!

My Other Mother

Dear Other Mother, I'm glad I have you
Because I love you through and through;
I want you to know that the very touch
Of your hand in mine has meant *so* much;
Your cheery greeting, "Well, how are you?"
Made many a day seem bright and new.
You'll never know how your wonderful smile
Has helped me travel each long, weary mile;
Each time I've been troubled or lonely or blue,
I've thought of you — you're *so* kind, *so* true,
So loving, patient, understanding and just —
The one perfect friend I know I can trust.
Each time that I've faltered along life's rough road
And grumbled a little because of my load,
It's been *your* smile that's set me — free;
It's been *your* faith that's made me — me.

A Mother's Part

It's a wonderful part each mother plays
  In this old world of ours;
She rules with just a kindly word
  O'er the great and mighty powers.

She builds our nations large and small
  With just a kindly touch
For she builds them in the very heart
  Of the child she loves so much.

This I Ask
(A Mother Prays)

Lord, give me a trusting heart —
Give me faith in Thee and in friends;
Help me find the pathway of hope —
The one that never ends.

Lord, give me happy feet,
The kind that never mind
Trudging the second mile
Ahead or yet behind.

Lord, give me willing hands
And the courage to see things through;
Beyond the call of duty
Let me pick the rose *and* the dew.

Pretty face? It matters not
For love will be shining there
Reflected from two hands and two feet
And one heart that has learned to care.

Still a Mother

In other days, in other years
I slept with one ear open;
I heard each small whimper that came from the crib —
I kept constantly prayin' and hopin'
It wasn't the measles, the mumps or the croup
Or even just one tiny sniffle;
I never kept count of the trips that I made
Just to pull up the cover a "triffle" —
Just to see that the crib's newest occupant slept
With full tummy contented and cozy,
But I guess, Lord forgive me, just once in awhile
I wished for a future so rosy
I could just go to bed and sleep the night thru
With no thought of a bottle or bubble.
"Oh, give me just one night to sleep," thus I'd muse,
"With no need to listen for trouble."

But now that there's only just Daddy and me
No reason to watch over the fretful,
The nights seem much darker, so lonely, so long
For somehow my ears are forgetful;
They still seem to keep thinking that in the next room
They should hear someone twisting or turning.
Does a mother no matter how wrinkled or old
Ever stop listening or yearning?

Poor Unfortunate Me
(For the Little New Mother)

I'm such a very unfortunate Mom —
Fate follows me all the day long;
I can't find my shoes, my hair just won't curl,
The coffee's too weak or too strong!
I get in the tub — some friend's bound to call,
Just listen to the telephone ring!
I slip on the rug at the end of the hall
And someone says, "Why don't you sing?"

Poor unfortunate me!

Whenever there's chicken or berries to sell,
The market report's way down low;
But then, when I go to buy those things, well,
I wonder why money doesn't grow.
I sit quietly down to look at TV,
The picture will flutter and flip
Or the plaster falls down from the ceiling on me —
Ev'rything I buy is a gyp!

Poor unfortunate me!

I wash a few clothes, the washer goes askew
And at least sixteen buttons pop off;
These things which I tell you really are true,
Dear reader, now don't you dare scoff!
I hang up the clothes, it's a beautiful day,
But the clothesline is sure to break;
I rush to the rescue, but Old Shep's in the way.
What a horrible mess he can make!

Poor unfortunate me!

If I water the garden or plan to go out,
As sure as you're born, it rains;
I try ever so hard not to bang things or pout
And what do I get for my pains?

I plant some new bushes and if they don't freeze,
I can't smell even one little rose;
I take just one sniff and either I sneeze
Or a bee stings me right on the nose!

Poor unfortunate me!

My bread never rises, my jam never jells
I scorch ev'ry nice white shirt collar;
I just get "sot" down and that sweet baby yells —
By now I could just let him holler!
I gulp down a pill and wish I were dead,
I feel so abused and forlorn;
I rush to my bed and — sure — I bump my head!
Oh, why was I ever born?

Poor unfortunate me!
Poor unfortunate me!

Like a Ship at Sea

Like a ship at sea that has lost her way,
I, too, wander aimlessly
About my house, my lonely little house
Now that my days are free.

Time was when these walls echoed far and wide
With laughter and music and noise;
Time was when my days were filled to the brim
With "doing" for my girls and my boys.

Like a ship at sea that has lost her crew,
My house is empty and still;
There's no need for stuffed turkey, chocolate cookies, or cake;
There are no empty tummies to fill.

Time was when arms ached from kneading fresh bread,
From sweeping and then sweeping some more;
But now it's my heart that keeps aching tonight —
There's no one to sweep the house — for.

Here's a Mother

God took the beauty of a dew drenched rose,
The warmth of the springtime sun,
The dainty perfection of white columbine
And rolled all these things into one.
He added pure faith, some love like His own,
The music of a gay meadow lark,
More courage and patience than found anywhere
Then He said to the whole wide world, "Hark!
Here's a mother! Here's a mother! Here's a mother!"
And my heart echoed, too, as all glad hearts do,
"Here's a mother! Here's a mother! Here's a mother!"

Vacation Time

Oh, I love the spring with its blossoms, don't you?
And even the winter, though chilly, will do;

But regarding the summer, I'm just not quite sure —
The whole month of August I can hardly endure!

There's mud and there's crumbs, there's dogs and there's noise
And dozens of neighbors — both girl friends and boys;

There's meals to be fixed and comp'ny galore —
When you are the "fortunate" mother of four;

There's washin' an' ironin' an' five beds to make,
An' then, when you've done this, you say, "Goodness sake!

I wonder why I have just two hands and feet
For there comes more comp'ny — an' I am just beat!"

More bakin' an' fixin' an' more pots of stew —
Oh, I love the spring with its blossoms, don't you?

But when comes the fall, I like *it* the best
For that's when we mothers of school children rest.

Everything Nice

It smells so good in our kitchen to me
But it's not like perfume, quite, you see;
It's more like soup and ham and rice
And a mixture of ev'rything that's nice.

My mother just loves to cook and bake
Anything from meatloaf to chocolate cake;
Our kitchen smells good because she's there —
She'd make things smell good, well, anywhere.

Need for Each

My Bonnie Lou's the bossy type
    While Mae's as meek as a lamb;
Cecelia's quite the clinging vine,
    The jolly one is Sam.

Ramona likes a frilly dress
    But Judy likes blue jeans;
The others eat most anything
    But Bobby just likes beans.

I'm sure if I had a dozen more
    No two would be the same;
Yet I wouldn't change a single one,
    In fact it's quite a game.

To find the best that's in each one
    And then help him do his part
To make and keep a happy home
    With love in ev'ry heart.

God Knew

God knew we'd need — a guiding hand,
  A loving heart to understand
When all the world was strange and new,
  For babies don't know what to do.
That's why He made — mothers!

God knew we'd need — a lullaby,
  A soothing voice if we should cry,
Two list'ning ears if we should wake,
  A kiss to heal each childish ache;
God knew we'd need — a gentle touch,
  Much more than a friend's, yes, twice as much
To make and keep us ever strong
  When we were tempted to do wrong.

God knew we'd need — a place to rest,
  The solace of a mother's breast,
The hope that she alone can give,
  Her blessing ev'ry hour we live;
God knew we'd need — a mother's smile,
  Two eyes to guard us all the while,
Two arms to comfort and to care,
  A love that no one else could share.

God knew we'd need — her help to walk,
  Her words to teach us how to talk,
Her faith to follow day and night,
  Her prayers to give us — second sight;
God knew we'd need — her patient way,
  Her loyalty day after day;
God knew we'd need — her love to teach
  The human things His hands can't reach.
That's why He made — mothers!
That's why He made — mothers!

A Special Task

A special task God gave to me —
    He placed within my arms
A child to call my very own,
    To guard from earthly harms;
A special task God gave to me —
    To teach this child what's good.
Lord, help me, I'm so prone to make
    Mistakes I never should.

The Extra Touch
(To Mom)

It's the cherry atop the ice cream,
It's the frosting on the cake,
It's the parsley atop the 'taters
That really seems to make —
The extra touch.

It's the flowers that line the sidewalk
That leads up to your door,
It's the bird's nest in the pine tree
That seems to make it more —
The extra touch.

It's the little deeds of kindness
You do to make me glad,
It's your special kind of lovin' —
The sweetest I've ever had —
The extra touch.

It's the way you go about it,
The extra second mile,
That somehow makes just livin'
Seem really worth the while —
The extra touch.

Mom's Pumpkin Pie

Pumpkin pie, Mom's pumpkin pie —
  The kind she used to bake!
Oh, how I wish I had a piece —
  Just for old times' sake.
To be sure my waist line doesn't need pie,
  Not even one small slice;
But pumpkin pie, Mom's pumpkin pie
  Was really *very* nice.

It came from pumpkins we had raised
  Out there in the fields of corn;
We boys and Dad used to haul them in
  On our wagon now old and worn.
The kitchen used to smell of spice
  On a chilly autumn day
When we came in, we boys, from chores,
  Or from our game of play.

Pumpkin pie, Mom's pumpkin pie!
  I can see it setting there
On the kitchen sink just to cool a bit —
  How I wish I now had my share.

The Handiest Things

Mothers are the handiest things
To have around, indeed,
Without mine I could never find
Well, half the things I need.
My pencil always seems to hide
Where I can't see it at all
And books have ways about them, too,
That never hear me call;
My shoes don't seem to be right where
I put them just last night
And papers that I need the most
Crawl clear beyond my sight.

But that's not all my mother knows
Or all she does for me;
She bakes me toll house cookies, too,
And peach pie, one, two, three.
She always has a dollar left
She's saved, yes, just for me
And when I'm feeling down and out
Or sick as I can be
She knows just what to do it seems
To make me feel all right.
Oh, a mother's 'bout the handiest thing
To have — come day or night.

Lost

It was just a little well worn path
Down at the end of the lane,
But it led to home and mother and peace —
Relief from each small childish pain.
I wandered by just the other day —
The lane was there all right
But the path had somehow disappeared
And mother was nowhere in sight.

There was no one but strangers inside the house
And they couldn't possibly know
Why I had gone there on this sunny day,
How great was my need to go.
Somehow I thought that mother would be there
Just as in days long gone by;
The ache in my heart she would understand
Without even questioning why.

But that little brown path that led to our door —
Well, it just wasn't there today;
And so, Mother dear, wherever you are,
Now I'll be on my way.

FATHERS

Thanks, Dad

I had the best dad in the whole wide world —
  None could be kinder than he;
He didn't give me all that I craved,
  But he gave what was best for me.

And all in all that was what I, too,
  Wanted more than anything,
To be the kind of son he'd like —
  Among my pals a king —

Not because of what my dad gave me
  But because of what I had earned;
True wealth is in proving one's own true worth —
  This I'm thankful I've learned.

And so, Dad of mine, wherever you are,
  Thanks for the things that you gave;
But thanks much more for teaching me how
  To work, to be strong, to be brave.

Yes, thanks for keeping the road a bit rough,
  There was foresight, I know in your plan;
Thanks Dad, for giving me ev'ry chance
  To make of myself — a man.

Dads Are Like That

Our dad wears faded and old beat up clothes
To work or to church or wherever he goes;
He drives an old car that's falling apart
And sometimes, alas, it won't even start.
He eats his meals home and says with a grin,
"It tastes mighty good but I've got to stay thin."
He saves ev'ry penny he can for old age
And thinks he's as wise as a prophet or sage.
But Junior steps out in a new suit and tie
The kind that is sure to catch a girl's eye;
He drives a sports car at ninety-five miles
And wonders each day why Dad never smiles;
He eats at a high fashion club or cafe
But guess who's the one that surely will pay?

He says, "My dad's great — he'll always provide
Clothing and shelter and money beside."
If only some saint could tell Dad today
'Twould be better if things were the other way.
But fathers, I guess, since this old world began
Said, "I'll give my son ev'rything that I can."
And so I can't change it even if I would;
But perhaps I should try. Do you think that I should?

Dad's Home

I'm home from work and what do I find?
  A book and my favorite chair?
The smell of fresh biscuits, roast beef or ham?
  And coffee filling the air?
No sir! All these things are but a dream —
  I can't bear to think of it now;
The baby's bawling at the top of his lungs
  And Tommy's having a row
With Tammy who's just turned twelve. She wants
  That "dreamy" TV act.
While Tommy shouts her down — for a time,
  Without one bit of tact.
And then there's Becky who's on the phone —
  She's been there, I'm sure, since three;
But yet she doesn't stop at all
  To say "hello" to me.

Poor Jennifer is in the room
  A playing at her scales
While mumbling it's the piano's fault
  If her history test she fails.
And Dottie, dear Dottie, my loving wife?
  She's gone to get her hair "done."
The P.T.A. meets promptly at eight;
  The president? Well, she's the one.

Home — from work — and what do I find?
  I'm just the poor silly dope
Who works all day to pay the bills,
  There *should* be enough cash — I hope.
Oh, well, they're happy, they're a normal crew,
  And what should I ask for more?
Somebody must keep them "normal" I guess
  And what are fathers for?

God's Gardener
(A Father's Prayer)

Oft times I kneel among the hilltop pine trees,
   In chapel fair, out underneath God's sky;
'Tis here I bring my ev'ry joy and sorrow
   To share with Him who lives and reigns on high;
'Tis here I see the wonders of God's garden,
   Through graceful boughs, like windows arched above;
'Tis here I sing with all God's lowly creatures,
   "I thank Thee, God for all these things I love."

And as my hands caress the velvet carpet,
   The eager shoots of precious lacy moss
Bespeak the care of One with matchless mercy —
   The One who died for me upon the cross.
The huge carved rocks that form my chapel doorway,
   The crystal spring that is my sacred fount,
The beaten path that leads to fields below me,
   These are among the blessings I can count.

Oh, I'm so glad the loving Master chose me
   To work out there among His growing corn!
What joy to feel the soft brown earth at seed-time,
   And know it's mine to till this very morn!
What bliss to watch the grain in God's own garden
   All sprouting forth in gladness of rebirth;
Each blade proclaims the resurrection story
   Fulfilled once more in all God's pulsing earth!

This be my pray'r, "Till ev'ning shadows veil me,
   Lord, may I ne'er betray Thy trust in me!
Oh, let me be a faithful, humble gard'ner,
   Who seeks to bring a harvest home to Thee.
Then with the dawn, O Lord, may I tend gardens
   In other fields, somewhere beyond the sun;
And may I sing Thy praise in other chapels
   Atop a hill, when all my work is done!"

Dad Baby-sits

Promise me you won't tell Flo
    And I'll tell you a secret or two;
She went to town and left me home
    With nothing at all to do —
Nothing, that is, but watch Cindy dear,
    Who's just turned one year old.
"Surely a man like you can sit,
    For she's as good as gold."
Those were my darling wife's last words
    Before she left me here.
She hadn't turned the corner — quite,
    Till me, oh my! Oh, dear!
I had to sit me on the floor
    And build a house of blocks.
I thought, "Now this is just my style,"
    But down, all down she knocks.
Then next we played I was a horse
    While she was the rider fair.
"Giddiap! Giddiap!" I can hear her still
    As we went round the parlor there.

That was O.K. but we had to stop twice
    For milk and orange soda, too,
And then for a pack of cookies all iced
    With chocolate. Oh, oh! Wheee-ooo!
The old wash cloth dripped, I knew it would,
    So we must change our dress.
All this and just ten minutes gone —
    I'm *tired*, I must confess!

Well, I don't know just how it was,
    But "dear Cindy" is in bed;
And don't you tell my darling wife
    A thing I ever said!

Pa Has the Rheumatiz

I've got the rheumatiz!
Ma has it, too, she sez;
But hers don't hurt like mine —
It couldn't — nobody's could!
Besides she's had hers too long,
It ought to be worn out by now;
Mine came just yesterday —
It's new and full of fire.
Oh, my! How can I stand it?
I've got the rheumatiz!

What Dad Can Do

When I was little, I confess,
My pockets were an awful mess;
I used to carry sticky gum
And stale fish worms and toads — well some!

But now my pockets turn out fine
I only carry fishing line,
My scout knife, this of course you know,
And fish hooks just in case I go
A fishin' in our little creek,
Then this thing here's my lucky stick.

My daddy carved it out for me
From a little branch of our maple tree;
It looks just like a wishbone, too,
Oh, there isn't *anything* Dad can't do.

Just Plain Me

To the folks uptown, I'm Mr. Success —
I'm loaded with wisdom and righteousness,
My suit's always pressed and my hair's just so
For these folks have learned to expect it, you know.
I must nod and say, "Yes" when they ask what I think;
I must act as if *their* jokes tickled me pink
But to the wee lad who climbs on my knee
And the others at home, I'm just plain me.

I'm just plain me, neither good nor bad
But I'm loved just because they can call me, "Dad."
I don't have to smile when I wish I could shout;
I don't have to laugh when I wish I could pout;
I don't have to tell them sweet words I don't mean;
I don't have to prove what they've already seen.
To the wee lad, my own lad, who climbs on my knee
And the others at home I'm just plain me.

I'm just plain me and I like it that way.
We all need some praise sometimes, but say,
I'm really not wise or righteous at all —
I'm even quite petty and mean and small;
I hate pretending I'm something I'm not,
Trying to give what I haven't got;
I'm glad to the lad who climbs on my knee
And the others at home, I'm just plain me.

If I

If I, in departing,
Can just leave behind
Faith pure and simple
Within someone's mind—
A suitable chapter,
A fragment of song
To ease bitter heartache
As time goes along,
Then, though the Reaper
Be swift or yet slow,
I'll not be mournful
When I, too, must go.

If I, in my living
Can work out some good
Or speak words of kindness
As all people should;
If I may bring hope
As a bright scarlet rose
To someone who sees it
Wherever he goes,
Then, though my petals
Shall wither and fade,
My life shall re-echo
Like a song softly played.

Ere I, in my living
Have reached the last mile,
May I do one thing, Lord,
A little worthwhile?

GRANDPARENTS

Now and Always

Come get your tea things, Kathy dear,
    For Nana wants to play;
She likes to dream as well as you
    Of some far distant day
When you're a hostess sweet and kind
    And she's a welcome guest —
Your heart, your home, your life — all these
    By God forever blest.

She Understands

A grandma's 'bout the nicest thing
A feller ever had;
She seems to understand and care
Even when I'm bad.

She never seems a bit surprised
When I fill my pockets with mice;
She never makes me wash my ears,
She never calls me twice.

She always sits and reads to me,
The kind of stories I like,
And she doesn't think I'm a bit too young
Even for a two wheel bike.

She bakes me cookies, the nicest kind,
With raisins and nuts stuffed inside;
And she never says, "Now don't eat too much."
She just lets me decide.

A grandma's 'bout the nicest thing
A feller ever had;
But I wonder why she says so much,
"Buster, you're *just* like your dad!"

In Grandma's Attic

Oh, I love to rummage in Grandma's attic!
There are so many things to see
Like old buttoned shoes and real funny dresses
That are much too tight waisted for me.
There's a big tall black hat, a nice long tailed coat,
And a vest — I guess you would say;
An old crooked cane and gray striped pants
That are oh such fun when we play.
There's a queer looking thing Grandma says is a churn
And three of those funny old lamps;
There's four of those great big heavy flat irons
And oceans of strange looking stamps.
But each time I go near a certain brown trunk,
Well — Grandma is sure to call,
"Now, dearie, those things are not for you."
I think it's her love letters and all.
Oh, I love to rummage in Grandma's attic —
'Specially on a rainy day;
I can hear the rain on the patched tin roof
And oh, it's such fun to play!

Grandma's Lap

My Grandma has the nicest lap —
It's soft just like my bed;
And when I sit there she will read
What Jane and Billy said.
I love to snuggle in her arms
When I'm too tired to play.
Oh, Grandma has the nicest lap —
I guess I'll stay and stay.

Granted Grandma

No one in this whole wide wonderful world
Could have so much fun — well not quite;
No one but a grandma, who else, pray tell,
Would dare to claim the right
To rock a dimpled darling to sleep
When she should be fed and put down?
Who else could see the look of her son
In each little smile or frown?

Who else could feed a child so much pie,
Cookies or chocolate cake?
Who else could find so much beauty in the things
Two little hands could make?
Who else could know the thrill it brings
To hear a child's voice say,
"Come, Nana, take me! Take me please!"
Oh, it's good to be a grandma today!

A Mother — Once

I wonder why all daughters feel
    That grandmas don't quite know
When Junior ought to take his nap
    Or just be rocked, like so.
I wonder why they can't quite see
    We know, sometimes, what's best
When it comes to oatmeal, cookies, or milk
    Or how warm he must be dressed.

I wonder how they think we raised
    A fam'ly of six or eight
Yet taught them all how to be polite
    And not leave food on their plate.
I wonder how they think that they
    Acquired their superior skill;
I'll never know, I'll just never know!
    I'm sure I never will.

My Grandpa

My grandpa thinks of the nicest things
    For boys like me to do;
We take our casting rods and go
    A fishin' the whole day through.
I never mind just sittin' still
    If I can be right where
My grandpa is along the creek
    For I'm sure the fish are there.
We take along a bun or two
    And some hot dogs to cook on the fire;
My grandpa is the greatest chef —
    No better could we hire.

Sometimes we take old Rover out —
    Just to let him take a run
Down where the meadow meets the pond
    And, oh, we have such fun!
He fetches me a stick to throw,
    Then chases it a mile,
Comes running back to me all wet
    But wearing a huge "dog-smile."
Sometimes we three play hide and seek
    Out where the woods begins;
But no matter how we plan and scheme,
    Old Rover always wins.

My grandpa knows what boys like me
    Are wishin' for, I guess,
For way before I ask him to,
    My grandpa, he says, "Yes."

Left to You, My Daughter

The whole of my diary is yellow with age;
Sometimes my old eyes can barely read the page.

But tonight as I gaze on the words I once wrote
My heart can't help singing a queer plaintive note.

How strange to look back on those days long gone by!
How strange and how diff'rent and I *can* tell you why!

With the eyes of a grandma I see it all now
And I wonder if this were that day, well, just how

Would I manage it all, would it still be the same?
Would I play the same way when I knew *all* the game?

The whole of my diary is yellow with age,
But still I'm not quite as wise as a sage —

I've done what I could, the best that I knew
And as for improvement — I'll leave that to you.

Grandma's Privilege

I thought that I was proud the day
   My baby came to town;
I'm sure I bragged and bragged some more
   And turned things upside down.
But let me tell you all just now
   I've seen the sweetest face
There is in all this whole wide world
   Or ever any place.
I've seen a rosebud, sure as sure,
   I've held her in my arms —
My grandchild, oh, she's sweet as sweet
   With all her subtle charms.
I never had the time or strength
   To really play with mine;
But now I'm sure a grandma can —
   Manage, well — just fine.

Prize Cake

My Nana lets me help her bake
Real cookies, cakes and pies;
She knows a three-year-old can make
A wonderful surprise.
We take some sugar and some milk,
Some raisins, too and flour;
We mix and mix and then we're done —
It hardly takes an hour.

My Pop-pop Can

When things get broke or bent a bit
Or really out of line,
Who, then, can quickly fix them up
So's they will work just fine?
When trains won't run or shovels dig
Or swings won't swing at all,
Who, then, can make them go again
In summer, spring or fall?

Why Pop-pop can! *My* Pop-pop can!

When I let Teddy on my bed,
His doggie feet all mud,
Who fixes it with Mom all right
And calls me little Bud?
Or when I'm 'fraid of anything
Like snakes or dark or noise,
Who, then, can chase the boogies 'way
For little girls and boys?

Why Pop-pop can! *My* Pop-pop can.

SONS

We're Proud

Did we ever tell you, Son, we're proud
Of all you are today?
Of all you've been throughout the years?
You're so fine in ev'ry way.

Did we ever tell you? Then I'll tell you once more —
You're the greatest joy we've had.
I can honestly say that we're both *mighty* proud
To be — your mom — and dad.

I Really Wanted the Best

I sat and I dreamed as I held you tight
Of a future for you that was worthwhile and bright;
I dreamed of the millions of fabulous things
You would do, for manhood always brings
Its wonderful store of strength and skill;
I dreamed of the place in life you would fill.

Many years have passed and quickly, too,
Now I sit and dream but with empty arms
For youth has lent you all of its charms
And it sent you a dream of your very own
That within your mind has lately grown.
Ah, yes, my child, perhaps it is best
And just as fine as any of the rest.
You must do, I know, what is in your heart
For this dream of yours is so much a part
Of all you are and soon shall be
Though it's all so very new to me.

How sweet it was to sit and plan
What things you'd be when you were a man!
But all I really wanted, I guess,
Was just your perfect happiness.

To a Grown Up Son

Oh, why must I sit helplessly by
Over there and pretend
You're tough enough when things get rough
Not to care?

Oh, why must I sit helplessly by
And not hold you to me
Once more, just once more as I've done before
When it's cold
And say, "It's O.K., Son — *everything's* O.K. —
Now!"

Parting

I smiled from the steps
    As I waved goodby;
But deep within
    My soul seemed to cry,
"It will never be
    Quite the same again —
He's gone to take
    His place among men."

I bore him and raised him
    The best that I could;
I often kissed him
    And said, "Son, be good!"
But now the world calls,
    Naught is left but to pray,
"Oh, please, God, go with him —
    Each step of — the way."

Just As He Is

I look down on a wee tousled head
Sleeping so cozily there in his bed;

Oh, what has become of that ear splitting noise?
It couldn't have been all the other boys!

Ah, yes, how I love him, asleep or awake,
In spite of the trouble and noise he can make!

I wouldn't change a thing, not one hair of his head —
Awake or asleep in his own little bed!

Eve and You and I

Oh, how Eve must have wept over Abel
    And wept again for Cain!
How full of despair and untold anguish
    Was *her* heart as the one was slain!
Yet, too, she must have been proud of Cain
    For other kindlier deeds;
She must have been torn between love and remorse —
    Between grief and concern for his needs.

It has ever been thus since the world began
    And it will be till life is done;
A mother runs the gauntlet of human emotions
    Each step goaded on by her son.
From the moment he draws his first fleeting breath
    On to each new success,
There is pride in each vict'ry, and in each defeat,
    Pure torture and yearning for redress.

Her heart may be broken in a thousand pieces
    Till faith comes to temper each fall;
But lives there and breathes a *mother, anywhere*
    Who *believes* it's not *worth it — all?*

You Must Choose

One day he's a captain that sails the high seas
   In a gay and wonderful style;
The next he's a doctor who mends broken arms
   With oh, such a sweet winning smile!

Then on to a fireman, a pilot, a chief —
   Each day he's somebody new;
Oh, I dream, too, little boy of mine,
   Some of these things just like you.

But I know I must lock my dreams in my heart
   For you must go your own way;
In the years to come you alone must choose —
   I can only wait and pray.

Miles and Miles Away

You're miles and miles away tonight,
   My little lad grown tall;
The years have made your shoulders broad
   And mine quite stooped and small.
And yet, and yet, I cannot help
   Wond'ring as I lie awake
Are you tucked in safe in your bed tonight?
   Who'll tiptoe in to take
Just one more look? Are the covers up?
   Your pillow arranged all right?
Your slippers set out beside your bed?
   Did you think to turn out the light?

You're miles and miles away, I know,
   But is there a mother too old
To wonder if her child is tucked in tonight —
   Safe from the chill and the cold?

Changing Hands

Tiny blonde curls all over your head —
So sweet, so adorable everyone said.

I heard this over and over again,
Then Daddy, one day, began to ask, "When?"

Those curls will just have to go, I guess
But somehow I can't bring myself to say, "Yes."

Give me just one more day to hold him, my dear,
Then bravely without shedding a single tear,

I'll let you and the barber see if you can
Make of *my* baby — *your* little man.

Mine at Last

I've never stood on a college hill
   And claimed it as my own and such;
I've never sat in a college class,
   But I wanted to, oh, so much.
I've never tasted the food for thought,
   The knowledge that fills the mind;
I've never found my answers in books
   The great intellectual kind.
I've never known the friendships that come
   From a common need and goal
Instilled in the heart of a young college girl;
   I've never had it — as a whole.

But I've shared it with you, my dear college lad,
   Each moment I've lived with you there;
I've gone to your classes, I've cheered at your games;
   In my heart I was everywhere.
And I'm glad, oh, so glad you could have all these joys,
   You could walk where doors closed for me;
You could learn all I wanted to learn from those halls;
   I'm so glad, *for you*, it could be.

To My Son
(On Graduation Day)

Dear Son,
What would you like most in life?
There are so many things that I would like to give you
If I were able.
But I am not able to go out and shop for the things
Which I would want most because, you see,
The things I want most for you can't be bought.
If I could rub Aladdin's lamp
And get only one gift for you, I believe,
From all the others, I would choose,
Faith —
Faith in your God,
Faith in those you love,
And faith in yourself.

This faith I cannot hand you, but I can hand you this
"Handbook of Faith," — the Bible.
Here is one for your own. It is not a new one,
It is *my* well worn one. In it,
I have found the faith which I hope
Will also be yours.
Search for it,
Diligently and daily, Son, and you will be sure
To find it. This will be my first gift to you
Because I hope you will always put God first in your life.
I hope you will always keep this little Bible with you
Wherever you go.
May it be a guide to you in times of indecision
A comfort — in sorrow;
A source of hope — in despair
And a constant joy to you in your daily living.
You remember I have always said to you, "Strive not
For greatness, but strive for goodness
And greatness will come to you."
So, may this little Book serve as a guide

In your future conduct, reminding you always
To do right, not because Dad and Mom said so,
But because God said so and because
It *is* right.

You will have many decisions to make in the future.
In the past —
Dad and I have tried to help you. I hope and pray, Son,
That you will see and understand that
What we have decided with you and for you has been
For your ultimate good. Before making
Any important decisions, always listen
For God's voice and then say, "Not my will
But Thine be done." God will always guide you if
You are willing to listen.

Second, if I could, I would give you a ring — not an expensive,
Dashing, bold ring, but a plain one with your
Initials on. Let it be a symbol of
Love never ending —
Christ's love for us all, our love for you and your love
For all mankind.
Wear it,
And wear it proudly, Son, for you can be proud
Of those initials as of now.
They stand for
A lad who is not rich but is willing to work,
Not great but willing to rise,
Not all wise but willing to learn.
They stand for a lad who
Is not only strong and brave
But kind and thoughtful, and above all
Honest and true. Let's *keep* it *that* way, Son.

Third, if it were possible, I would like to give you
A camera. Dad and I will be missing you dreadfully.
Life won't ever be quite the same without you around
With fish hooks in your pocket, papers strewn
All over the floor, and cookie crumbs in a trail
Behind you. Please send us pictures of your life so that
We can feel we still have a part in it. Then, too,

I can tell by the expression on your face
That you are happy — and that is all
I need — you happy in the service of God and those
You love and all our fellowmen. That is —
A king's portion.

Fourth, I would like to give you a wallet — not brim full
But sufficient for your ev'ry need. Then, don't forget
The first portion belongs to God, the Giver of all
Good things. After that, your wallet will
Always stay slightly filled if you remember
What Grandpa used to say, "It's not so much
What you earn as what you save." To this
I might add, "Good management consists in buying the things
You want most
And letting the rest alone."

Fifth — now here is a silly gift!
Silly?
It's just a cake of soap!
But, to me, it means more than keeping your face clean,
Although that's important, too. Let it be
A symbol of a clean life — So live,
That you can face anyone, anytime, clean, unafraid
And unashamed.
This has turned into quite a sermon, hasn't it? But I'm
Pouring my heart out to you; I'm saying all the things
I wanted to say to you down through the years when you
Were young and I could tuck you in at night. I hope
At least some of these words will echo
On through the years as you grow older. I hope
You will still hear them re-echo
When my voice is no longer here to utter them.

The last gift I would give you, if I were able,
Is a set of cuff links and a tie clasp.
Can you figure what they are to mean
To you? Yes, of course! Clasp your hand
In that of God's; link your life to
That of His and to those of good companions.
Evil companions can do more to ruin one's life

Than anything else I can think of. Choose carefully
And pray — pray without ceasing. Never be ashamed
To pray and, someday, when you stand
Before your Maker, He will not be ashamed of you. Sometimes,
You may think that your prayers are not
Answered. Then be sure to see if you are trying to push
Your will on God. If you are, you must stop and wait
Patiently
Until He speaks. Of one thing you can be sure —
God's way is the best way.

As I have said, would that I could
Give you all these gifts wrapped in a little package, Son.
The package would be marked, "Happiness" and would contain
Faith, love, joy in service, physical comfort, cleanliness of
Heart and mind, and — good companionship.
But, you see, the only gift I have actually given you is
This Handbook. From it
You will learn how you can get all the other things
For yourself. These things
Cannot be given to you by anyone. You must
Seek them out
For yourself.
God bless you, Son.
Love,
Mom and Dad

Mother Is Right

I can't see why mothers don't like pretty snakes;
They don't hurt a thing, for goodness sakes!
I don't mean the big ones, just the kind in our yard,
They're those little green thin ones, but I'll try real hard
To please my mother with all my might
For Dad's always saying, "Your mother is right."

The Perfect Rose

I wear a blossom in my hair—
Betwixt the gray you'll see it there!
You'll see a gem, a golden crown,
The one put there by hands of brown,
Strong hands that once were baby pink,
Strong hands that cared enough to think
Of mother on her special day
And honor her in a special way.

I wear a blossom in my hair—
Kind thoughts from one who said, "I care!"
His love the gem, the golden crown—
Today I'm a queen of great renown!

I wear a blossom in my hair—
Betwixt the gray you'll see it there!

Our Bowser

There once was a doggie, our dear little Bowser—
    He was just an old toy, yes, it's true,
With green button eyes and funny old whiskers
    And his long blackish hair all askew.
But how dear he became to a gay little laddie—
    His constant companion was he;
What secrets they shared, this wonderful couple!
    What good times were yet to be!

There once was a doggie, our dear little Bowser.
    And I reckon there still is today
Up there in an old wooden trunk in our attic
    Where Bob put him safely away.
No power on this earth could make me disturb him,
    Our Bowser a sleeping there,
For tucked in beside him are millions of mem'ries
    That no lonely mother could spare.

First Day at School

Today's not like any other day —
The dishes are washed and all put away;
The beds are all made, the curtains in place,
Pajamas all hung up, even flowers in a vase;
The rooms are all dusted, all shining and neat
No marks on the oilcloth of small muddy feet;
No clamor and noise — just the tick of the clock
And a lump in my throat that's as big as a rock,
For this morning my baby, my pride and my joy,
Skipped merrily out down the street — a new boy.

Just once he looked back as I watched from the door
And my arms ached to hold him, cuddle him once more.
Was there just one small tear in his eye do you think?
I can't be quite sure for quick as a wink
He turned and went galloping on down the street,
On down toward the schoolhouse and the new friends
        he'll meet.

I think in that moment he grew deep inside
Toward the man he'll be soon in the world, oh so wide
Toward a height that can never be measured in years
Or yet in the flow of a fond mother's tears.
Today's not just like any other day —
The schoolhouse seems farther and farther away.
Won't four o'clock come? Won't four o'clock come?
And this is the day I wished for, well — some.

All a Part of Boys

Fishin' hooks an' worms an' such
All around the place!
Why anybody steppin' in
Might think it a disgrace!

But fishin' hooks an' worms an' such
Are all a part of boys
As well as baseball bats and gloves
An' lots of other toys.

So fishin' hooks an' worms an' such,
These things we've got to see
But it's only for such a little while
For soon a man he'll be.

Sauce for the Gander

There's just one thing in this old world
I'll never understand!
In a voice that purrs my husband says,
"Now isn't that just grand?
My son is on the honor roll!
My son is in the band."

But when *our* son does something bad,
He's sure to boldly shout,
"Do you know what *your* son has done?
He's knocked a window out!"
Now tell me — why should he be cross
When I play *turn about?*

You Can Tell

From the attic to the cellar
  You can tell a boy lives here —
There are fish hooks by the dozen,
  Rod and reel is lying near.
There's a bike outside the window,
  Torn gum boots wait on the porch;
Bent tin can of worms beside them
  And a funny kind of torch;
There's a stack of airplane models
  On his bed and on the floor;
Plus the glue and knives and trinkets
  In a box behind the door;
All the walls are filled with pictures
  Of each kind of dog there is,
But the mud that's on the carpet's
  From that straggly dog of his;
One new bow complete with arrows
  Fills the corner over there
Next a million other doodads
  Like a hammer and a square;
Catchers' mitts and big league baseballs,
  Flashlights, test tubes, in a row
Fill his closet shelves completely
  And each inch of space below.

In the attic there's a tractor
  And a wheelbarrow that's broke,
Battered firetrucks, trains and engines
  That once ran and that's no joke;
Horses, horses, blocks and marbles,
  Lincoln logs and red toy drums,
Yes, and here's a game of checkers
  And a yellow top that hums.
Look! I've found some leaden soldiers
  And a fleet of ships, it's true,
Down beneath that Indian headdress

In a chest that once was blue.
Hanging high along the rafters
   There's a net that used to be
Kind of handy as a gadget
   To catch butterflies for me.

In the cellar there's a jig saw
   And a jar of pickled snakes —
I must stop while I've the patience
   And the fortitude it takes
Just to wade through, straddle, walk round
   All the things my son holds dear —
From the attic to the cellar,
   You can tell a boy lives here.

Strained Baby Food

Strained baby food — I'm sure it's fine,
   At least I think it is;
But Johnny, who is just six months,
   Has ideas that are his.
The vitamins that it contains
   Don't mean a thing to him;
He doesn't care a bit, mind you,
   If he's fat or stays quite thin.
Each spoonful meets a stubborn tongue
   Or else a bobbing head,
Or even madly waving arms
   Lest he, by chance, should be fed.

Ah! Now he's done it! Um! That's great!
   He's grabbed his near full dish
And set it squarely upside down
   Upon his head! — I wish —
But I had better not say what
   I wish would become of strained food;
I'll wait awhile and perhaps I'll find
   I'm in a better mood.

It's No Use

It's no use! It's no use!
  Oh, how many million times
Have I picked up the toys
  On the floor?
Yet each time I turn
  My back for awhile,
Our Tommy appears
  With some more.

It's no use! It's no use!
  There are blocks a mile high —
He's found them again,
  I confess;
There are trucks from the porch
  To the parlor and back
And under the bed,
  I guess.

It's no use! It's no use
  To clean up again;
He'll use my new pan
  For a drum;
He'll play kitchen chairs
  Are his hide out or else
He'll find where I've put
  My gum.

It's no use! It's no use!
  I'll just have to wade
Around
  And over his blocks.
Will he never grow up
  Will he never grow up?
Oh, give me a toy chest
  That locks.

Will I Ever?

Will I ever find a towel
  In the bathroom, hanging neat?
Not a finger mark streaked down it,
  Yet the washing — all complete?
Will I ever find the flip top
  On the toothpaste — as I ought?
Will I ever find shoes shiny
  As the day that they were bought?
Will I ever see a puddle
  That John Jr. won't wade through?
Will I ever see a sport shirt
  That's as clean and good as new?
Will I ever, will I ever
  Live to know he's combed his hair?
Will I ever? Will I ever?
  Now this minute, I declare —
He was looking in the mirror,
  Making faces — at himself
And I thought I even saw him
  Put the comb back on the shelf.
Then, perhaps, there's hope tomorrow
  Or the next day, maybe three;
Will I ever? Will I ever?
  Guess I'll have to — wait and see.

I Understand

I never could quite understand
    How one little tiny smile,
Two rosy cheeks, two outstretched arms
    Could ever in just a short while
Make such a change in two young lives;
    I never, that is, until
I saw that smile, those cheeks, those arms
    Of that little tyke called Bill.

He came to live with us, you know
    And now our world revolves
Around his ev'ry stretch and coo,
    The problems he daily solves.

I used to sleep till half past eight
    And never care if the clothes
Got washed till the middle of the afternoon,
    This, ev'rybody knows.
I used to take a coffee break
    Well, ev'ry hour or two,
Brush out my hair and dress myself
    In a style that was really quite new.

Big Bill never used to hurry home,
    He never helped with a dish,
He never even seemed to think
    I had a single wish.

But now our lives are diff'rent, quite —
    I hustle all day long;
There's this to do and that to do
    To raise Bill good and strong.
I never could quite understand,
    But now I know a lot
And Big Bill, too, he's changed his ways
    For the little tyke we've got.

Five Copper Pennies

Five copper pennies — and what will they buy?
He thinks he's a millionaire
As he starts down the road to the country store
Without a frown or a care.

Five copper pennies and a light in his eye!
This is my little lad,
The one with brown eyes and the blonde curly hair
And the lips that never look sad.

Five copper pennies and his mind on the mints
That I know he loves so well;
The store is a castle where a fair princess waits
With pink ones and white ones to sell.

Upside, Downside

I never could quite understand
Why there is two of me;
When mother says do this or that,
My one self won't agree.

The other self stays quite polite
And answers, "Yes, I will";
And yet a tiny little voice
Says "Son, think twice, be still."

I'll never understand it quite
How I can be so bad
When really only one of me
Could ever make folks sad.

Don Chandler

Mrs Reah
274 9770

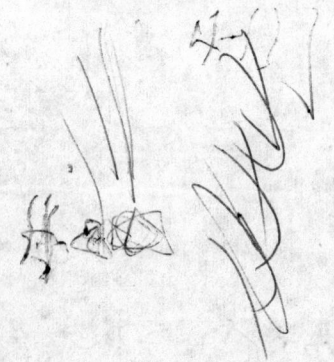

DAUGHTERS

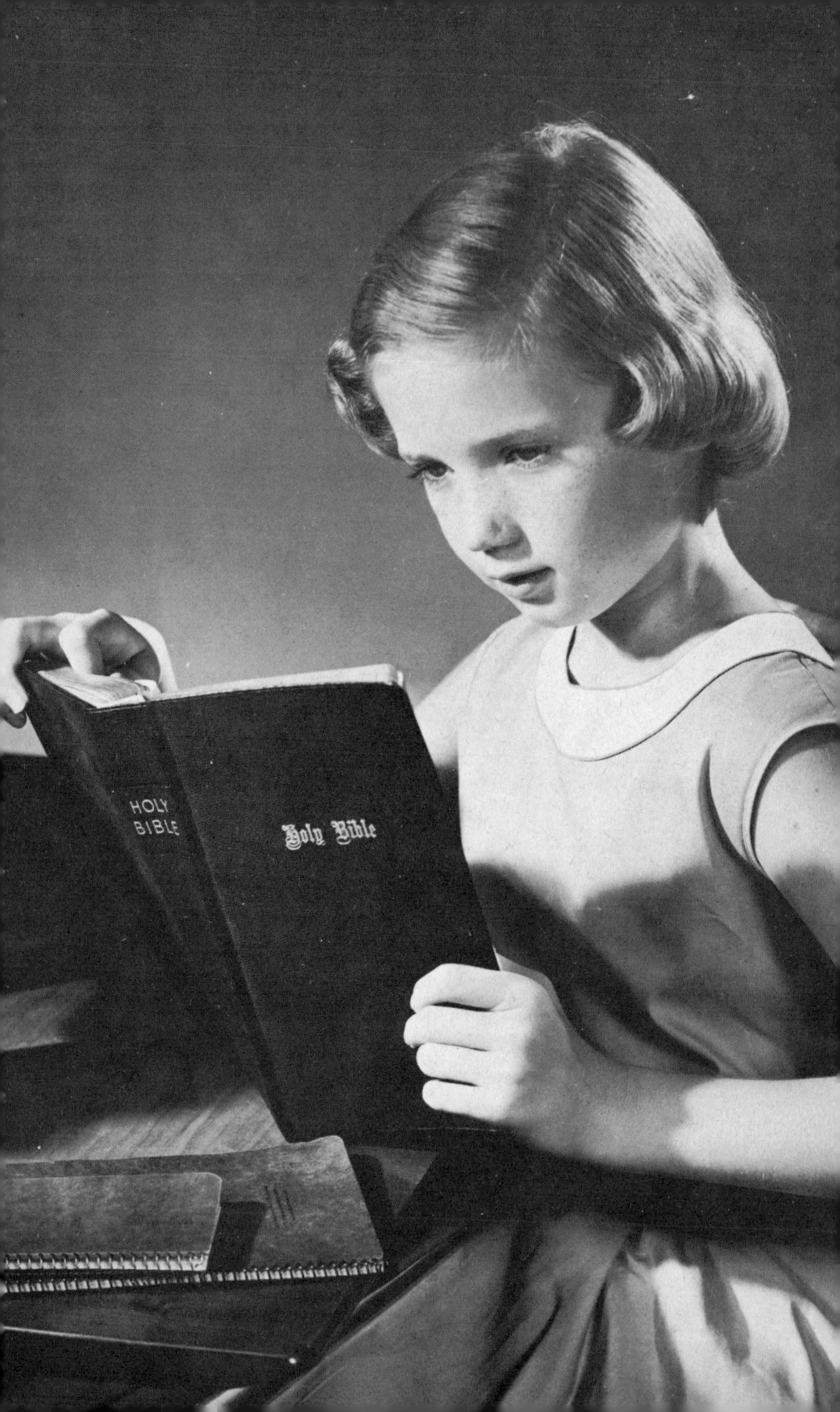
HOLY
BIBLE
Holy Bible

A Thousand Million Questions

There's a thousand million questions
That my daughter wants to know —
In the middle of the summer
When it's hot, why can't it snow?
How can little bitty brown seeds
Into red tomatoes grow?
How do dark clouds up above us
Bring the rain just like they do?
Why does grass grow all around us
'Stead of just a blade or two?
Why do doggies bark to wake us
While Sue's kittens only mew?

There's a thousand million questions
That my daughter wants to ask;
Is it, then, dear Lord, too brazen
Since to answer is my task,
That I beg, oh, please don't let me
Wear a grim forbidding mask;
Let me spare a workday moment
To learn more about such things,
Give me wisdom, daily wisdom,
From Your secret hidden springs —
There's a thousand million questions
That my darling daughter brings.

Filling My Shoes

There is just one thing Melinda,
  Though she's only half past two,
Seems to like above all other
  Things she sees her mother do;
When she's quiet for a minute,
  I just know I soon shall hear
"Clip-clop, clip-clop" from the closet
  And then very, very near.

High heeled slippers hold some magic
  For her pudgy little feet;
She can "clip-clop" in her fancy
  Where all stately ladies meet.
I can tell by looking at her
  That her mind's nowhere around
In the closet or the kitchen
  Where her twice clad feet are bound.

She's a lady of distinction,
  Quite a belle, a village queen
Far more priceless in my slippers
  Than most anyone I've seen.
Wear the slippers, dear Melinda
  But don't trip again and fall;
Take your dreams and go a walking
  Through the parlor, down the hall.

Soon you'll be a fine young lady
  Wearing just my style and size;
Oh, I wonder in that moment
  Will I know what's good and wise?
When you fill my shoes, dear daughter,
  Will the things I say and do
Be a good enough example
  For a grown-up queen — like you?

To the Future

Some day, when you're old and wrinkled, gray
And as wistful, my new daughter, as I am today
You, too, may possess a fine grown up son
Far dearer to you than most anyone,
Then, and then only will you understand
For you will have dreamed and worked and planned.
Perhaps on that day in your heart you'll forgive
If need be, and love me as long as I live —
Love me *because* I have loved my son, too,
Loved him *so* much, oh, if *you* only knew!

Some day you *shall* know, of this I am sure
For you'll have a son, and your love will endure
Then my foolish ways you'll no longer despise
For you will be seeing through a fond mother's eyes.

Just Could Be

They all come back to me now that I'm gray —
The things my mother used to say.
They seemed so foolish and old fashioned then
But that was back in the good old days when
I was eighteen and she was gray —
That was a diff'rent, oh, a far diff'rent day.

But they all come back to me now as I look
Beyond the things I read in a book
For now I'm the one who's old fashioned and gray,
The one with the daughter who knows the way
Things ought to be done or ought to be said,
Things I can't seem to get into my head.

But I'm quite content knowing some autumn day
When she is the one who's old fashioned and gray,
She, too, might remember things about me —
She, too, might have a daughter, well, mightn't she?

My Dream Came True

No other dream so completely possessed me
    As that of a little girl —
A girl I could call my very own daughter,
    A pure and genuine pearl.

Little girl of my dreams, you're mine, my treasure
    And you're perfect, just as perfect as can be;
Today as we sit here I just can't help thinking
    "I'm *so* glad you belong to me."

A Girl and Her Dolly

A girl and her dolly, they belong together,
    Just the same as butter and bread;
She's a wonderful mother if I ever saw one —
    She's in earnest from her feet to her head.

Forgetting herself, she cares for each dolly
    With capable, untiring care;
To her not the beauty, but the need of each dear one
    Determines the time she must spare.

That's why poor Minerva whose hair is all straggly
    Gets combed and combed over again;
That's why her dear Patty who's forever hungry
    Is fed, though she just *had* been.

The dolly she takes when she snuggles in dreamland
    Is never the prettiest one;
It's just Mary Jane, the one who might need her
    When her prayers are over and done.

A girl and her dolly, they belong together —
    I guess God made them that way;
In her heart she's the same little loving mother
    You are in *your* heart today.

May I Share?

I have no little girl of my own,
    No child to cuddle or squeeze;
No sweetheart to read to or to buy pretty dolls,
    No angel to try hard to please.

But I saw such a little one just today —
    She moved in the house right next door
And oh, if her mother doesn't care, I'll pretend
    She's what I've been praying for.

I wouldn't want to ask her to call me "Mom" —
    I'm sure just "Auntie" would be fine;
She looked so sweet in her ruffled pink,
    Do you think she would like to be mine?

A Lady Quite Fine

I know I'm old fashioned, real grumpy and fat,
Little daughter of mine, little daughter of mine!
But won't you forgive me today for all that?
I'd like to be truly a lady quite fine.
A tall stately lady without hat askew
Walking beside you in satin and lace.
But pray, what do you think "Your Highness" would do
With no chocolate chip cookies or pie in the place,
Yet dishes piled high in and over the sink,
No clean skirts and blouses to hang in a row?
Please tell me, my darling, just what would you think
When you're all bathed and manicured, ready to go?

I know I'm old fashioned, real grumpy and fat,
Little daughter of mine, little daughter of mine!
But won't you forgive me today for all that?
I'd like to be, for your sake, a lady quite fine.

Little Red Rocking Chair

There's a little red rocking chair there by the fireplace
　That's oh, so empty tonight;
A little blue-eyed girl once sat there rockin' —
　The proudest mother in sight.

In my dreams I can see her with her curly haired dolly
　She's rocking while the "baby" sleeps,
Singing words that only a mother's heart
　Knows or ever keeps.

There's a tiny red rocking chair there by the fireplace
　Waiting for someone I know;
But the little blue-eyed girl that once sat there on it
　Was a part of the long, long ago.

Little Pink Blanket

I have a pretty pink blanket, I do
And I love it, oh, so much,
Not because it's pretty or even pink
But because it's so soft to touch.

When eight o'clock comes and my mother calls,
"It's time to go to bed!"
At first I think I'd rather play
With Minerva Ann instead.

And then I remember my fav'rite thing
And I go, yes, right away
For it's oh, so nice to snuggle down
With this blanket when I'm tired from play.

As Her Mother

I can see her sitting there in her little rocking chair
  Sewing dresses day after day;
Her dolly had to have each dress like her own
  Or as near as it could be that way.

Tiny stitches and some big ones I happened to see,
  But her dolly won't care, I know;
Mother love shone clearly even then on her face —
  In the good old days — long ago.

Now my daughter still rocks but in a middle sized chair,
  Still sews little dresses pink and blue;
Beside her sits *her* daughter with *her* needle and thread
  Sewing like her mother used to do.

Perfect Daughter-in-law

Little daughter-in-law! Little daughter-in-law!
I can't tell you all you mean to me,
But I couldn't love you more if you were my own —
This I am sure you can see.

I wish I had known you long, long ago
When you were but two or three;
I'd like to have held you then in my arms,
Close, oh, so close to me.

Little daughter-in-law! Little daughter-in-law!
You're so thoughtful, so sweet, so true,
So perfect for us all, even Daddy and me —
Let me thank you for being ——— you.

My Favorite Recipes

I have some favorite recipes
    Dear little daughter of mine;
My mother gave them all to me
    And I'll pass them down the line.
They may not seem of much worth to you —
    I remember I, too, felt like this;
But I'll pass them down and one day you'll see
    They're something you should not miss.

There's her chili sauce and her cherry pie
    Her crisp ginger cookies, too,
And her special kind of dark fruit cake,
    Well, just to name a few.

But down at the bottom of each recipe
    In mother's own writing it reads,
"Just add with the other ingredients here
    All the love that anyone needs;
Mix it well with good humor and plenty of hope;
    Add a prayer for those who partake;
Then serve it with kindness and joy all around —
    What a wonderful feast it will make!"

Yes, these are my favorite recipes,
    Dear little daughter of mine;
My mother gave them all to me
    And I've passed them down the line.

Stars That Are Mine

There are stars tonight not in the sky
　　Yet they twinkle and twinkle at me;
They're within the eyes of a tiny girl —
　　One who has just turned three!

There are stars tonight like diamonds so rare,
　　But yet more precious their glow;
I'm sure they reflect God's wonderful light —
　　He sent her to me, you know.

Along the Selfsame Way

A watchful eye I ought to keep
　　On all I do and say;
A little child is walking close
　　Along the selfsame way.

She marks each word she hears then tries
　　To use it as her own;
She even imitates my style,
　　My color and my tone.

I see her acting out a play,
　　This little mother, too;
Her Raggedy Ann gets told each day
　　Each thing she may not do.

I see myself in her ev'ry act,
　　I hear my ev'ry word
In simple things I thought for sure
　　She never even heard.

A watchful eye I ought to keep
　　On all I do and say;
A little child is walking close
　　Along the selfsame way.

To Each Her Own

Daughters, dear daughters, no words can express
What wonderful joy, what true happiness
God gave to us mothers when He sent you here
Into this world where you've all grown so dear.
Your eyes may be dark, your eyes may be blue,
But God found the place, the *right* place for you;
He put you, each one where you'd be loved most
He chose, this we know, so forgive if we boast.

Don't you wonder how God, even God could have known
How dear to each other we'd be ere you'd grown?
Daughters, dear daughters, we love you, each one
But we'll each take our own girl when all's said and done.

All Unheard

I'd like to tell you all the mistakes
   I've made on *my* pages of life;
I'd like to guard you from all these things,
   From all the pain and the strife.

I'd like, daughter dear, to give you advice,
   I'd like to smooth your way;
How my heart aches that you, too, must learn
   All by yourself someday.

But daughters, I guess, can't hear very well,
   Or heed is a better word;
For ever since mothers were mothers I'm told,
   Daughters have seldom heard.

While You Wait for Me

She had angel blue eyes and raven black hair,
This child I once called my own;
Her skin was as white and as pure as her soul,
Pure as any I've known.
And oh, I wanted her so, God knows —
Why did she have to go?
It was thus I mused in the still of the night,
Then suddenly out of my woe
I saw her standing at the top of a hill,
The sun shone over her head;
But her dear little face was turned toward the west
And my sad heart was filled with dread
My heart so stricken with new-born grief
For I saw bound around her feet
Huge chains which were holding her back
As she stumbled on that golden street.

Then only for a second, I glimpsed on beyond
A meadow where children played;
I heard angel voices, I saw those sweet smiles —
What a wonderful sight they made!
But a voice I knew as that of my child
Called oh, so sadly to me,
"Please, Mommy, oh, please let me go, let me go —
These chains are your own, you see.
I cannot come back and I cannot go on
Where it's oh, so pretty, Mommy dear;
I want to play with the others over there
And it looks so very near.
Just throw me a kiss and wave good-by
And my chains will be no more.
Hurry, Mommy, for I'll have more fun over there
Than I've ever had before."

I didn't know, God, how You loved my child
With her eyes of angel blue;
I love her, too, and because I do,
I give her just now to You.

Let her join the others in the meadow so fair
There where she wants to be;
I shall shed no tear from this day forth;
Run play, dear, while you wait for me.

Dreams Do Come True

A lace bureau scarf formed your first bridal veil
    When you were only three;
A bunch of bluebells your bouquet —
    A pretty sight to see.

A pretty sight for on your face
    You wore a childish grin
And there was frosting from the cake
    All around your little chin.

But deep within your eyes I saw
    A dream that grew and grew;
And today in your satin and chantilly lace
    I saw that dream come true!

Today Is the Day
(To My Daughter)

Don't cry about mistakes you've made,
But use them as a test;
Don't fret about some future task,
But give today your best.

Yesterday has come and gone
As each tomorrow will,
So fill today with faith and love
For God is with us still.

The Child Left Out of the Game

I stood and watched the children at play,
I saw her as she came,
The little girl with the faded dress —
The child left out of the game.

I wanted to gather her close in my arms
Though I hardly knew her name;
I planned to wipe the tears from her eyes
And whisper, "What a shame!"
For oh, what queer twisted legs she had,
And how very, very, lame!
But I thought I saw a smile on the face
Of the child left out of the game.

Though life has been very good to me
And I've only myself to blame,
I must confess I have sometimes felt
Thwarted in ev'ry aim.
That's why I wanted to comfort this child,
Light a spark from my feeble flame;
But I looked again at the tiny face
Of the child not quite the same
And I saw anew that wonderful smile —
A picture any artist would frame!
She seemed really *glad* the *others* were not
The child left out of the game!

So now, when I feel all life's joys are gone
And there's nothing left to claim,
I remember and I, too, am glad I can be
The child left out of the game.

Another New Dress

Another new dress? *Another* new dress?
  You have at least sixteen!
Why don't you wear the yellow one —
  Your newest one, I mean.

It's far too long? Too out of style?
  You bought it just last week;
You loved it then, 'twas just your kind.
  And now? It's quite a freak?

Another new dress? *Another* new dress?
  Dear little daughter of mine,
The purple one with velvet top
  I'm sure will look just fine.

Um! *That* old thing? You wore it once?
  I know you did, but then
It looks so nice I'm sure you could —
  Wear it once again.

Another new dress? *Another* new dress?
  Well, I guess I wanted one, too,
With pleated skirt and top like Jane's
  When I was young like you.

God Hears

We knelt beside her little crib —
My Kathy Ann and I;
The prayer she prayed was very short,
But I'm sure it reached God's sky.

"Dear Jesus bless us all tonight
Amen," was all I heard
But for a child so new from heaven
God stoops to catch each word.

REFLECTIONS

My Borrowed Girl

I've never had a little girl
With golden curls and big blue eyes;
I've never bought the little frills
That bring a squeal of glad surprise
Like dolls and petticoats and things
All full of ruffles, lace and such,
All colored pink, a dainty shade;
But oh, I've wanted to so much!

I wouldn't trade my laughing boys
Their bikes and trains and overalls,
Oh, no! I never could do that!
But just for today, if someone calls
And asks me if I'll baby sit
I'll *have one* for a little bit!

I could pretend for just this once
We'll play the nicest kind of games
With dolls and dishes and tiny stoves;
I'll sit right there and think of names
To call the food we have for tea.
Then I'll hold her on my lap and read
Of little fairy princesses.
I'll rock her till she sleeps. Indeed
I'll hold her just a little while more
And in those moments, oh, so brief,
I'll know the love a mother feels
For her tiny daughter. Each joy, each grief
I'll share with her though I speak not a word.
I'll just hold her close and kiss her hair.
A dream, of course, but oh, how sweet!
My borrowed girl! My answered prayer!

Our Task
(Sunday School Teacher)

I always did like frilly dresses
    And little girls who wear them,
Black patent slippers and little poke bonnets
    And mothers who gladly share them.

I breathe a prayer ev'ry Sunday morning
    To the wonderful God above us
Who sends to this world and to all its churches
    These little angels to love us.

Somehow it seems to make life worth more
    Just to see these little visions
Of what tomorrow in its glory shall bring us
    When *they* shall make the decisions.

Oh, yes, these tiny tots shall soon be —
    The mothers of a new generation;
How great, then, our task to give them a faith that
    Will build a better nation.

Any Mother Can See

Little girl with the freckles and the pink turned up nose,
Does anyone love you the less?
There's a wonderful mother out there in some home
I'm sure God sent you to bless.

There's nothing but beauty in any child's face
As any true mother can see.
Little girl with the freckles and pink turned up nose,
I just wish you belonged to me.

The World to Me

One day the Lord in mercy looked down
On a tiny house in our quiet little town;

He saw that I needed someone to love
So He sent you down from heaven above.

Your eyes were brown but they sparkled like dew
And two precious dimples you brought along, too.

Your tiny blonde head lay cradled in my arm
And from that moment on nothing else held charm.

You were my world, my ev'rything
And whatever the future years may bring,

Be it ever so great, so grand, so new
I wouldn't exchange it for one moment with you.

How Slow?

Measles, mumps and whooping cough,
　　These and many more
Of childhood's great catastrophes
　　I've met and calmly bore.
Did I say calmly? No, I guess
　　Those days were never calm
But when one has to face a thing
　　You do it without a qualm.

Indeed those days slid into years
　　And when they've gone their way,
You wonder what took so much time
　　And what you did all day;
You wish you'd done more of this or that—
　　Why didn't I? I don't know;
For I remember thinking that our Ann
　　Grew oh, so very slow.

Hand Me My Cane

Hand me my shoes and hand me my cane,
I must be a walkin' back home again.
I've traveled this world twice over, I guess,
And still I've found no place to comfort and bless
Like the old fam'ly homestead I left long ago
When my feet weren't weary with trouble — and slow.

Hand me my shoes and hand me my cane —
I must be a walkin' come sunshine or rain.
I've got to go back to that old country shack;
I'll follow the lane with my dog and my pack;
I'll find it, I know, standing all alone there
But I hope Mother's watching and waiting—somewhere.

Just for Today

Lord, make me a child once again, I pray,
Make me a child — just for today.

Let me find my mother in her rocking chair
With outstretched arms a waiting there.

Let me snuggle once more within those arms,
Let me feel, Lord, safe from all earthly harms;

Let her place her kind hand on my feverish brow;
Let me hear her say, "It's all right now!"

Oh, please let me tell her I've done my best,
Then let me stay there awhile just to rest

For oh, this old world is not what it seemed
Long years ago when I only dreamed —

Happiness seems so hard to find
And oh, I'm *so* tired in body and mind.

Lord, make me a child once again, I pray,
Make me a child — just for today.

My Poem

I thought to paint the sunset's gold,
  The purple of the mountains below,
A lake nestled peacefully there at the foot
  To mirror the depths of its glow.

I thought to sing a melody sweet
  Yes, sweeter than any yet heard;
The wealth of its tones would capture the heart
  Like the sweet, plaintive song of a bird.

I thought to write a beautiful verse,
  A page for the whole world to see,
A thing that would bring to many a soul
  New hope like spring to a tree.

But the sunset has faded and my brush is still dry,
  The song I once dreamed of still waits.
The poem? That, too, sleeps deep in my heart
  And closed are Time's heavy iron gates.

Yet, out on the lawn aromping with Wags
  There's a picture that's fairer by far —
My own little girl, my own little boy,
  Not on canvas, but just as they are.

There's a song, too, out there, a merry little song
  Sung in *their* style, not my own;
But it's sweeter, much sweeter than any I planned
  There's magic, true magic in its tone.

The verse? That, too, shall be written with care,
  But not with the stroke of a pen;
My words? The faith these small ones shall bring
  As they walk and talk among men.

All in a Day

When life is young, we dream fair dreams
  Of things that are to be;
When life's at noon, we live those dreams
  In all their reality.

When life's at twilight, soft and gray,
  We dream fair dreams once more;
But now they're filled with secret springs
  Of the joys that went before.

A True Millionaire

No matter how tiresome my work day has been,
  How cross, how untrue were my friends,
What peace fills my soul as I reach my gate —
  That moment my heartache ends.
Home! How I love ev'ry chair, ev'ry dish,
  Ev'ry carpet though it's faded and worn,
The old-fashioned lamp on the table over there.
  And even the curtain that's torn.

Home! There's some need for repairs, I know,
  But *that* doesn't matter at all;
I walk through the door and I feel I could hug
  The old clothes tree that stands in the hall.
When I've had me some supper and I'm in my old duds,
  I wouldn't change places with kings
For problems that looked big as mountains today
  Seem now just trivial things.

Home! How I love ev'ry room, ev'ry nook!
  What secrets these walls and I share!
How quickly they change all my fear into faith!
  Here, I'm a true millionaire!

If I Could Step Backward

If I could step backward just one step tonight
Back through the years in their swiftness of flight,

To a little white house at the end of the lane,
Mother would dry all my tears once again.

If I could step backward just one step right now
I could find the true faith that I've lost somehow —

The faith of a child, the pure, simple kind
That questions not, yet is never blind.

If I could step backward just one step awhile
And see once again my mother's sweet smile,

This grief would be easier far to endure;
I could feel, indeed, once more secure.

Have You Forgotten?

Have you forgotten how to laugh
The laugh of a merry child?

Have you forgotten how to pray,
"Lord, keep me pure and mild"?

Have you forgotten how to trust.
Implicitly trust — in God?

Have you forgotten how to see
The beauty in the paths you trod?

Have you forgotten how to forgive
And live with your fellowman?

Then you'd better go back, far back, through the years
And be a child again.

A Woman's Day

What makes a day complete?

The gold of the sun as it greets the earth?
The dew on the rose? Gay laughter and mirth?
A house full of servants? A trunk full of clothes?
The hundreds of things a wise man knows?

Oh, what makes a day complete?

The bright cheerful song of the meadow lark?
A walk in the woods or a day in the park?
A smile on the face of an old time friend?
The promise of gold a plenty to spend?

But what makes a day complete?

The beautiful sunset from your own front door?
Perhaps! Perhaps, but there's *so* much more.
It takes perfect faith in the One up above,
The patter of small feet and a husband to love.

This makes a day complete
This makes a day complete!

Finis

I'm writing "finis" to a chapter in my life —
"Finis" — it's over and done;
But oh, how clearly each detail remains —
How much it's a part of one.

I'm writing "finis" to all I hold dear
And I do it because I must;
How fondly I'd cling to one moment more,
But Time, I am told, is just.

Already I see before me new tasks,
New chapters in the book I now write;
Time has but to turn the pages for me —
Till tomorrow — "finis — goodnight."

Buckwheat Cakes 'n' Sausage

Hot buckwheat cakes 'n' sausage — a meal fit for a king,
No modern food can top them, not even anything.

When all the chores were over and I pulled up my chair,
I used to find them waiting beside my elbow there.

Hot buckwheat cakes 'n' sausage, a meal I can't forget;
It lingers in my mem'ry — a taste I long for yet.

But this welcome king style breakfast belongs to another day;
Home, my boyhood and sausage have gone, gone far away.

Oh, THIS *I'm Thankful For*

If there's one thing I am thankful for
Much more than other things,
It's the fact that I shall always have
What a certain mem'ry brings.

A many a day I sat and read
Beside my mother's knee
And always from God's precious Word —
This joy still clings to me.

By the kitchen window in the sun
Or by the old porch door
I sat and read at mother's knee
Oh, this I'm thankful for.

A many a time when things seem hard
I think of Mother there
And peace once more comes o'er my soul
As it did by the old rocking chair.

If there's one thing I am thankful for
Much more than other things,
It's the fact that I shall always have
What a certain mem'ry brings.

Just to Belong

Just to belong to someone who cares,
Just to know there is someone who shares
All of your heartaches, your joys and your prayers,
This is really livin'!

Just to belong, yes, just to be
A part of it all — just to say "we"
Just to speak of "my folks," not just "me"
This is really livin'!

Just to belong, just to feel the need
Of someone to comfort, to clothe and to feed,
Just a little hand to safely lead,
This is really livin'!

Just to belong! Just to belong!
Just to have faith in someone who's strong
Who will pull together as you go along,
This is really livin'!

Just to belong! Just to pick up the toys
Of my own little girls and my own little boys,
Just to give all the things the other enjoys,
This is really livin'!

Just to belong! Just to really know
There's someone who loves me and will tell me so
Even on days when my faults plainly show,
This is really livin'!

Whose Garden?

The garden is planted, there's onions and lettuce,
    And radishes, red ones and white;
It's raked over smoothly and patted down softly —
    As yet not one weed is in sight.
Oh, the joys of a home and a gay springtime garden
    Can't be told to a city man — quite.

All the time you are digging and scratching and planting
    You think of the corn that will grow;
In your fancy you see it stand taller and taller
    Ripe ears growing row after row.
How sweet it will taste when it's fresh from the garden —
    No city man ever would know —
That is unless sometime he plans to stop by there —
    Just happens to pass your fine place
The day when it ripens all ready for roasting —
    He just wants to see your kind face;
Never, oh never to show his new weeder
    Or even Ruth's dress of new lace.

The garden is planted, the onions and lettuce,
    Ah yes, and even the corn;
Although my back aches till I think it will kill me
    And my shoulders and arms feel forlorn,
I'm sure, to me, this corn will taste better
    Than to any man anywhere born.

More and Merrier

The ironing's piled a good mile high,
   The dishes are in the sink,
My head's in a whirl, I don't know quite where
   To begin — I can't even think.

The fam'ly's been here — they've been here, and gone,
   The boys, their wives and the kids,
Their dogs, their bikes, their strollers and such
   And everything protocol bids.
There's not one straight corner upstairs or down;
   We've moved ev'ry bed, ev'ry chair
For Billy's new play pen and Jamie's best coat
   Must be pushed or just hung over there.
The house, I am sure, weighed a ton or two more
   The minute they came here to stay;
The rafters, the studding, I'm sure heaved a sigh
   As soon as they went on their way.

Yes, the ironing is piled ev'ry bit a mile high —
   There's work ev'rywhere that I look;
But nowhere in all this wide world could I find
   A happier, merrier nook
Than here, yes, right here at home with them all
   Around us — together once more;
I'd do it all gladly again and again —
   I *think* — as I wave from the door.

Will I Never Have Time?

Will I never have time?
  Will I never have time?
This dirge beats and beats
  In my breast;
There are dreams like a crysallis
  Waiting to burst
And they writhe like a thing
  Possessed.
But there's work to be done,
  Yes, a huge endless stream,
A stream never calm now
  Or free;
It dashes and splashes
  Again and again,
Pushing me on
  Toward the sea.

Will I never have time?
  Will I never have time?
This dirge beats and beats
  In my breast;
It beats from within
  And the stream beats without
Its own urgent call
  Irrepressed.
Hope like the lamp
  In a lighthouse still burns
But dimmer and much
  Farther west.
Will I never have time?
  Will I never have time?
This dirge beats and beats
  In my breast.

Fit for a King

In all the stores uptown or down
Wherever I may roam
And even on my well stocked shelf
Here in my modern home
There is *no* food that can compare
With the one dish we used to get
When we went vis'tin' at Grandma's house.
Oh, I can taste it yet!

Home made ice cream with berries on top —
Not the usual kind
But that which was made from warm fresh milk
And the berries that we could find.
We used to take a little tin pail
And walk up over the hill
To where the berries grew wild and sweet
There by the old saw mill.

From the ice house we chose a big piece of ice
To put it in a burlap sack;
Then we broke it into just hundreds of bits —
You had to have the knack!
We turned and turned the freezer by hand
Till we couldn't turn it anymore,
Then we'd race to lick the paddle clean —
Each bite was better than before!

Home made ice cream with berries on top!
This was fit for a king!
If I could ask Old Man Time in his flight
To bring back just one little thing,
I'd ask to sit outside once more
In the shade of that old apple tree
With six big dishes of berries and cream
Right there along side o' me.

On the Bars of the Pasture Gate

Oh, to be sittin' once again
On the bars of the pasture gate
With nothin' to do in the whole wide world
But just to sit and wait!

With nothin' to do but to dream day dreams,
To wiggle my toes an' all that,
To feel the warmth of the midday sun
As it bypassed my old straw hat!
Each day I watched the small shadow there
That was me upon the ground;
Each day I whistled an old folk tune
And oh, what a merry sound!

I listened entranced to the lark overhead,
To the ripple of the brook near by
With now and then the soft welcome tones
Of a cricket or a katydid's cry.

Oh, to be sittin' once again
Watchin' old Bess and Kate
With nothin' to do in the whole wide world
But just to sit and wait!

Springtime Has Come

Springtime has come in all of its glory
  I can feel it, it's in the air;
Robins sing gayer, skies seem more blue —
  There's happiness ev'rywhere.

Springtime has come in all of its glory,
  Whatever the weather outside
For a dear little stranger with eyes like my own
  Has come to our house to abide.

Take Me Back Tonight

Take me back tonight, take me back, far back,
  Oh Time, in your ceaseless rush!
Take me back for just one moment more,
  Back beyond all this hush —
Back beyond all these useless days,
  Back beyond empty years
To the hour little hands clung to my own,
  As I shared childish joys and tears.

Take me back tonight, take me back, far back,
  Just for a moment or two!
Let me hold in my arms my baby once more,
  Let me hear her gurgle and coo!
Take me back, oh Time, take me back, far back
  To those long ago priceless days,
To the joys one vainly tries to replace
  In oh, so many ways.

Sharing the Years

Twenty-five years! Twenty-five years!
Has it really been that long
Since we walked down the aisle as one
With love in our hearts and a song?

Twenty-five years! Twenty-five years!
It seems only yesterday
For still, to me, you're as fair as then
And as sweet in ev'ry way.

Twenty-five years! Twenty-five years!
Like a stream they've quickly passed;
But they've left fond mem'ries in our hearts
Each dearer than the last.

Chicken 'n' Dumplin's

Chicken n' dumplin's and warm apple pie —
We're down on the farm at last
To visit with Mother and Dad and the boys
And live again in the past.
Upstairs in the darkness of my old iron bed
I can listen to the eaves drip, drop
And dream of riding down mulberry lane
In a surrey with a fringe on top,
The one I love seated close by my side
Pretty and laughing and gay
Unmindful of trees or sky or brooks —
The happiest of the happy that day.

I'm a berry stained, barefoot boy once again
Dreaming these beautiful dreams
I can hear my dad as he called back then,
"Get up, it's most daylight, it seems.
It's time to go milk and feed the cows
And give those old horses their hay!
Get up, my son, get your lantern lit —
There ain't no time to play."

Chicken n' dumplin's and warm apple pie
Fresh sausage and buckwheat cakes,
These were among the things on our plates —
What a lot of them, too, it takes!

How my toe seems to hurt where I stubbed it that day
Down by the gate near the barn,
And I hear Dad say as he used to say,
"Well, Son, won't you ever *larn?*"
Yes, I've stubbed my toe a million times
As I've walked life's treacherous road
And Dad's words keep coming back to me
As I trudge along with my load.

Chicken n' dumplin's and warm apple pie —
We're down on the farm at last
To visit with Mother and Dad and the boys
And live again in the past.

The Little Red Schoolhouse
(Fond Recollections)

The little red schoolhouse with its windows so bare
Its poor sagging steps and door
Still stands at the very top of the hill,
Still stands, but not as before.
Once gay childish faces peered out through each pane
Till the bell rang out, "School's called!"
Then Old Rover, too, sought a place inside
And not even the teacher looked appalled.
The seats were worn smooth and wide enough for two
Each desk had an inkwell on top
Just right for dunking those long yellow braids
Till the teacher called to us, "Stop!"

We kids were much more like a fam'ly than a class
For we came in assorted sizes
From five year old Nan to size sixteen Ned
And each day was full of surprises
Like the frog we put in the teacher's desk
That jumped right out in her lap;
Or the time we boys went swimmin' in the creek
And almost got the strap.
Oh, those were the days when pot bellied stoves
Were always a welcome sight;
It was golden enchantment just to watch the flame
Through the cracks where it wasn't tight.

What wonderful fun we used to have
At an old fashioned spelling bee!
How my heart would flutter when 'twas time to choose sides
Hoping "someone" just chanced to name me.
Oh, those were the days with no sign of a bus
Or a teacher for each single grade;
Now the little red schoolhouse with its poor sagging steps
Looks lonely, deserted, dismayed!

Log Cabin Style

What fun it is on an autumn night
To snuggle down in bed
And pull my old log cabin quilt
Up close around my head.
I think kind thoughts of Sally Brown
My mother and Sister Sue
And all the other folks that came
To see what they could do
To lend a hand at our quilting bees
In the days of long ago,
In the days when friends had time to sit
With other folks and sew.

I wonder why we're so busy now?
Much too busy I'd say!
There isn't time to quilt anymore
Or to pass the time of day.
It's bustle here and bustle there
And each one for himself,
The good old days and the good old times
Have been put away on the shelf.

What fun it is on an autumn night
To snuggle down in bed
And pull my old log cabin quilt
Up close about my head!
The love that went into each stitch,
The pure unselfish kind,
This love has kept me cozy and warm
And brought me peace of mind
Through many a day and year since then
Through many a joy and tear —
What greater gift than the gift of love?
What mem'ries half so dear?

The Old Nine Patch

Up in our attic there's an old faded quilt,
It's one of the nine patch kind;
It's been there for many a year, I guess,
But it isn't too hard to find.
You open the lid of the old brown trunk,
The one that was Grandma Kate's,
And there on the top neatly folded away
The nine patch patiently waits.
I'm sure that quilt dreams that some day once more
It will cover some happy pair
For someone with kind loving hands one day
Tenderly put it there.

It was made from just left over calico
I'm sure I could pick out each block
That each neighbor brought to join to the rest,
I remember who wore each frock.
And oh, I remember the day they all came —
Mom called it a quilting bee.
She set up the frames by the living room stove
And pinned on the lining, you see,
The one she had made from the bleached salt sacks
Next the batting and the beautiful top;
There were chairs for twelve and soon they were filled
With the folks who had time to stop.

What fun they all had and how the time flew,
But the stitches were even and neat
For each woman knew her stitches would show
When the nine patch quilt was complete.
Such laughing and talking, such quick nimble hands!
How I wanted to help them sew!
But my job was to thread the needle and such
Till my eight year old hands should grow.

Then came the dinner and oh, what a feast —
Sauerkraut and dumplings and pork
With plenty of pie, yes, pumpkin and mince
And cake to eat with a fork.

Up in our attic there's an old faded quilt,
It's one we don't use, you see;
But what can a store bought blanket tell
Of the joys of a quilting bee?

This and Nothing More

You may talk of your little white cot in the lane
With roses that twine round the front door;
But my home was a tumble-down three-room flat —
This and nothing more.
Yet, oh, how dear were those rooms to me
For Mother was always there;
She could make it seem like a wonderful home,
Well, just about anywhere.
We didn't need a palace on top of a hill,
A golden throne or a robe;
We knew my mother was a queen all right —
The best on the face of this globe.

Somehow the barest, the most commonplace room
Took on a cozier look
When Mother was around for a little while
To sweep, to dust and to cook.
For ev'ry little thing she ever did
Was done in the spirit of love;
Nothing was ever too much work for her,
It was all a blessing from above.
Even our apartment three flights up
Was nearer heaven she said;
And so you may talk of your cot in the lane —
But I had Mother instead.

At Apple Parin' Time

When the year's at apple parin' time
And the frost lays on the ground
Then my thoughts go back, yes a good piece back
When old friends were all around.
My thoughts go back to a cozy room
Where the stove was shiny and black,
Where chairs were plain and worn and old,
But where love felt no sense of lack.

When the year's at apple parin' time
I see those chairs all filled —
There was Mom, Aunt Bess and little Mae
And love flowed so free that it spilled
From each face and it seemed to adorn the room
Like gold in that lamp lit place.
All fingers flew as they pared and cored
Those Winesaps as if in a race.

When the year's at apple parin' time,
I feel the crisp, cool air;
I see the bonfire out by the barn
And two huge black kettles there.
The men brought wood or sat and stirred
Around the welcome fire
Until the applebutter boiled up thick
According to their desire.

When the year's at apple parin' time
I think about these things
And wish that I were there again
With all the joys it brings.
I think about, well, this and that
And wish that kids today
Could go to just one apple bee
In the same old fashioned way.

Time Was

Time was when I longed for the city
With all of its bustle and noise
Just as a youngster longs for
Those precious Christmas toys.

Time was; When I stepped as lively
As any who walked the street;
I was one of the crowd and I counted
That day a special treat.
I hustled along through the market
And oh, what sights I would see —
Jewelry and furs and dresses
All waiting there just for me!
I thought to myself, "Well, someday,
I'll come back and buy them all,
Someday when I've made my first million,
Someday the city will call."

Time was and today I am farther
From that million than ever before
But somehow those things don't attract me —
It's God's country that I adore.

Time was when things that were store bought
Seemed oh, so attractive to me —
But that was before I discovered
The riches of a cool shade tree.
Oh, yes, I'd rather wear gingham
Than the prettiest pink lace gown;
I'd rather just wiggle my bare feet
In the sand than go to town;
I'd rather by far go walking
Down by the meadowland creek
Than jostle my way through the dime stores
Well, just to take a peek!

Time was! Oh, how swiftly it travels!
It's left me *far* behind,
But today I'm *really* seeing —
Time was — when I was blind!

Just an Old Stone Fence

I walked beside the old stone fence,
The sky was dull and gray
And the weeds beneath my feet grew tall
In the field where I used to play.
Ah yes, long ago it was that I
Called this my special fort,
A broken branch from the apple tree
Made a cannon of the finest sort.

How well I remember when the fence was laid,
Kind neighbors from every side
Lent a hand and we picked each stone from the field
To build it three feet wide.
Old Jebson Crane and Dan Van Dyke,
These were the strongest of the men,
They hitched Ned and Barney to their own stone boat
And loaded it again and again.

The air was gay with laughter, I know
And many a friendly shout;
I was far too young to understand
What the game was all about
But I felt the warmth of those neighborly smiles
I can still see those toil worn hands,
I can still see the patches on those blue overalls
I can hear Dad's gentle commands.

I can still smell the scent of the clover nearby
I can still breathe the same country air;
I can turn toward the west where the sun used to set
Like a diamond on the mountain's hair.
But the path that leads to the old red brick house
Is hardly a path at all
For the brush and the vines have done fine through the years
In their race to grow nice and tall.

Oh, to clasp hands with those friends once again —
Friends who were tried and true,
Friends who were willing to labor all day
Picking stones for the likes of you.
But I walked beside the old stone fence,
The sky was dull and gray
And the weeds beneath my feet grew tall
In the fields where I used to play.

A Little Bit o' Work

If I live to be a hundred years
I'll never have more fun
Than I used to have at huskin' bees —
I'd never miss a one.
What grander sight than a huge barn floor
Heaped high with shocks o' corn
It meant a little bit o' work
As sure as you are born.
But what's a little bit o' work
When it's done for a lifetime friend?
And somehow work don't seem like work
When the autumn's near its end
And other neighbors come by, too,
In an old fashioned buckboard and rig.
Why in just two hours we could husk enough
For ten cows and one brood pig.

If I live to be a hundred years
I'll never have, well, not quite,
That wonderful feeling of peace and good will
I had on a huskin' bee night.
It seemed that we worked not each for himself
But all with true love in our hearts;
And work is never real work, you see,
Till love from your task departs.

The Huskin' Bee

When the frost was on the pumpkin
And the birds had flown away,
Then 'twas time again for huskin'
And you'd hear my father say,
"I must get that corn in, Mother,
So as we can have a bee."
And she'd answer, "Yes, sir, Father,
Any night's all right with me."

Shocks of corn soon filled the barn floor,
There were lanterns hangin' high
As we hurried with the milkin'—
Folks would soon be droppin' by.

Then the sturdy rafters echoed
With their laughter and their song
And the hours of work went quickly,
They were never very long.

I remember, I remember,
Oh, how well I see it all,
I was then a lad of twenty
Brown of face, but straight and tall,
I was huskin' with the others
Then I shouted, "Look, red ear!"
And I held it high then higher
Though my knees felt kinda queer.
Ev'ry face turned toward Miss Sally;
Oh, just see her smile and blush—
She's the fairest at the party,
You could almost hear folks hush.
I went forth and claimed *two* kisses,
What a happy pair we made
As right there at the same huskin'
Springtime wedding plans were made.

Swingin' on the Gate

What fun I used to have each day,
  A swingin' on the gate
Down by the road 'neath the old apple tree —
  What a wonderful place to wait!
Soon Dad would come around the bend
  With the team and a load of hay;
Enchanted, I'd run to meet him there
  And then we would ride away —
Away to the barn and the old hay mow
  Where I would romp and play;
Away to horizons so new and so fair —
  Away, away, away!

If I could go back to my childhood days,
  Though Dad were ever so late,
You'd find me there 'neath the old apple tree —
  A swingin' on the gate.

Mended Dreams

My dreams lie crushed at my feet
Like a bruised and withered flower
With petals here and there.
And yet, till this very hour,
The perfume lingers on —
It lives and constantly taunts me;
It follows me night and day
As if it were meant to haunt me.

My dreams lie crushed at my feet,
They are scattered all about;
I can never gather the petals
But somehow, I do not doubt,
As Time goes rushing by
It will swish them up in the air
And carry them straight to you —
Hope — like a bud, new and fair.

[159]

Through the Years

The bells rang out and I said, "I do"
Twenty-five years ago;
They've been marvelous, fruitful, happy years —
Your love has made it so.

A down through the years I knew for sure
I could always count on you;
A' down through the years I knew without doubt
You'd be there when I needed you, too.

The bells rang out and oh, what joy
They've brought to you and me
For a down through the years our marriage has been
All we dreamed it would be.

Golden Years

Hand in hand you've worked and planned
    For fifty golden years.
'Though some days were glad and some were sad,
    You shared both joy and tears.

Sometimes 'twas he and sometimes she
    Who needed a helping hand,
Yet each was there to banish care
    With a love that could understand.

You've often said that flames which were red
    Burned out ere the night was through;
But flames which were blue were steady and true
    Like the love that you two knew.

Thank God above for this blue flame love;
    For the years you shared with each other;
For this event, and for what you've meant
    To us, dear Dad and Mother.